Jugular Vain

A Comedy in Two Acts

By
Paul Kerslake

Leschenault
Western Australia

Copyright Information

(See also page iv)

© Paul Kerslake 1991
All rights reserved.

ISBN: 978-1-923020-05-4
Published by Leschenault Press, 2023
Leschenault, WA Australia

Rights of performance by amateurs is controlled by Leschenault Press on behalf of the author and they, or their authorized agents, issue licenses to amateurs on payment of a fee. **It is an infringement of the Copyright to give any public reading of the play before the fee has been paid and the licence issued.**

The royalty fee is subject to contract and variation at the sole discretion of Leschenault Press.

The publication of this play does not imply that it is necessarily available for performance by amateurs or professionals, either in the British Isles or Overseas. Amateurs and professionals considering a production are strongly advised in their own interests to apply to the appropriate agents for consent before starting rehearsals or booking a theatre or hall.

For all performing licensing requirements or queries contact in the first instance: legal@leschenaultpress.com or call: 0061 43 909 5500

Jugular Vain

First produced as a two-act play by the RAF Wyton Players, Cambridgeshire on 4th November, 1993 with the following cast of characters:

The Count:	*Iain Slater*
Roderick:	*Dave Veal*
Siobhan:	*Wendy Selleck*
Clemency:	*Julie Worrall*
Rebekah:	*Amy Burt*
Gunther-Gunther:	*James Langridge*
Kevin:	*Bob Kretowicz*
Debbie:	*Zoë Turner*

Produced by Nick Jones
Setting by Geoff Phillips
Directed by Ian Hooper

Revival produced by the Bunbury Repertory Club, Western Australia on 21st July, 2023 with the following cast of characters:

The Count:	*Rob Littlewood*
Roderick:	*Ron Tait*
Siobhan:	*Abby Ross*
Clemency:	*Kym D'Ath*
Rebekah:	*Kate Martin*
Gunther-Gunther:	*Brandon Forsyth*
Kevin:	*Brodie Simms*
Debbie:	*Clare Simms*

Produced by J R O'Shaughnessy
Setting by Charise D'Ath
Directed by Ian Hooper

Copyright Information

(See also page ii)

This play is protected by copyright. All rights, including Stage, Motion Picture, Radio, Television, Public Reading and translation into foreign languages are strictly reserved.

The right of Paul Kerslake to be identified as author of this Work has been asserted by him in accordance with sections 77 and 78 of the Copyright, Designs and Patents Act 1988.

No part of this publication may be reproduced, stored in a retrieval system, copied in any form or by any means, electronic, mechanical, photocopying, recording or otherwise transmitted without written permission from the publisher. You must not circulate this script in any format.

This dramatic script is a work of fiction, and any resemblance to actual persons, living or dead, is purely coincidental. Acknowledgment is made to the inspiration of Bram Stoker and his original publication, Dracula, Archibald Constable and Company, London, 1897.

License for amateur performances are issued subject to the understanding that it shall be made clear in all advertising that the audiences will witness an amateur performance; that the name of the author of the play shall be included on all announcements and on all programmes; and that the integrity of the author's work will be preserved.

The Royalty Fee is subject to contract and subject to variation at the sole discretion of Leschenault Press.

Video recording of performances. Please note, any intention to video record ANY section of the performance for ANY purpose whatsoever must be cleared by obtaining permission from Leschenault Press in advance. Video rights are NOT granted as part of a standard performing licence for this play.

Dramatis Personae

The Count: The one and only, original, Count Dracula – 600 year old vampire who has turned over a new leaf, become vegetarian and is trying to move into the modern world and not kill people.

Gunther-Gunther: The Count's faithful servant of 600 years. Quite disappointed at the Count's new leaf.

Roderick Peters: Deplorable business executive without any perceivable ethics or morals, in business or love.

Siobhan Bibelot: Roderick's secretary. Having an affair with her boss.

Clemency Hoyden: A sassy American 'eco-warrior' who is verbally combative at the drop of a hat.

Rebekah Douay: A religious zealot, out to rid the world of vampires.

Kevin: Newly wed to Debbie. Easily scared thrill seeker. Alternatively, with little changes to script, can be Debbie's son.

Debbie: Newly wed to Kevin. Easily scared thrill seeker. Alternatively, with little changes to script, can be Kevin's Mum.

SYNOPSIS OF SCENES

Act I – The Sword Room, Count Dracula's Castle.

Act II – The Same. The next day.

ACT I SCENE 1

SCENE – *The Sword Room: Count Dracula's Castle. Afternoon, but all curtains are drawn shut.*

Roderick and Siobhan are on stage.

Roderick: *(Confronting an imaginary vampire, his fingers making the sign of the Cross)* Begone, foul demon of the night, creature of darkness! Return to your lair or be vanquished! Stealer of souls, corrupter of the innocent, devourer of the pure! Flee! Black Prince of Hades, begone! Perdition awaits you! *(Quieter)* What do you think? Good?

Siobhan: That's not very funny, Mr Peters, someone might come in.

Roderick: Scared?

Siobhan: No.

Roderick: Yes.

Siobhan: Maybe.

Roderick: Yes!

Siobhan: YES!

Roderick: Thought so. *(As caricaturist, once more)* Fear not, sweet Angel. For while I have these two trusty fingers *(making the sign of the Cross)* I promise that no cold-blooded neck- biter will touch you.

Siobhan: So, what are you doing all weekend?

Roderick: Smart arse.

Siobhan: Sorry.

Roderick: Why not here? Now? The curtains are shut.

Siobhan: Someone might come in.

Roderick: Never stopped you at the office.

Siobhan: Well… I'm not in the mood.

Roderick: Never stopped you at the office.

Siobhan: But it's spooky.

Roderick: It's meant to be spooky. We're in a Transylvanian castle, for Chrissake. Who saw the brochure? Who thought it might be fun? Who booked us in here for the weekend? I only paid for it.

Siobhan: I know, and I am grateful.

Roderick: How grateful?

Siobhan: Well, lots.

Roderick: So?

Siobhan: I want to go home. Or Paris. I could be saucy in Paris.

Roderick: You can be saucy here, right?

Siobhan: But what if… you know… there really are… things? Here in the castle?

Roderick: Things?

Siobhan: You know. (*Quietly*) Vampires?

Roderick: (*Loudly*) Vampires? Night-stalking vampires? Blood-chilling, heart-gripping, spine-locking vampires? A vampire coalesces from a column of mist in our moonlit bedroom, to the far-off sound of a tortured wolf. (*He mimics a wolf howl and coughs*) The creature becomes substance as you sleep, wracked by strange and horrifying dreams. Its red eyes fix on your naked throat. If only you had worn your small, silver cross, a gift from your dear Aunt. Not for you, then, this terrible fate.

Siobhan: Mr Peters, you're frightening me.

Roderick: Hush! The tall stranger, dressed like midnight, glides silently across the room and pauses, savouring its delightful anticipation, before stooping over your pale, anguished form. The ghoul's thin red lips part, revealing pointed fangs gleaming wickedly in the moonlight.

Siobhan: No!

Roderick: Yes! (*Pause*) But wait! Brave Roderick Peters, asleep at your side, stirs and, suddenly free of the death-like stupor that had cloaked his mind, senses peril. He turns, faces the danger and, without a thought for his own safety, leaps at the monster!

Siobhan: Get him, Mr Peters, get him!

Roderick: The desperate pair fight; Roderick's dauntless courage barely a match for the ferocious vampire's inhuman strength. Suddenly, the vampire gains the upper hand and throws our hero across the room where he lies bruised and breathless (*falling in front of the fireplace*). The foul creature advances, victory in its malevolent smile. Only one thing can save Roderick and his companion. Do you know what that one thing is?

Siobhan: (*Shakes her head furiously*).

Roderick: As the monster moves to place his powerful hands around Roderick's throat... The Cross!

Siobhan: Hooray, Mr Peters!

Roderick: (*Advancing, arms outstretched*) Begone, Prince of Darkness!

Siobhan: (*Applauding*) Hooray!

Roderick: I command it! Leave us (*processing around the stage*), and fly into the night on your dark errand. Begone, I say, begone!

(*Roderick is now facing the door as Gunther-Gunther enters, opening the door on Roderick's outstretched hands*)

Roderick: Ow! Damn! Blast! Ow! Ow!

G/G: Assistance?

Siobhan: You bashed him with the door. (*To Roderick*) Does it hurt?

Roderick: I think they're broken.

G/G: Most fully contrite. Proximity unexpected.

Roderick: I'll say it was unexpected.

G/G: Injury?

Roderick: Injuries. Both hands.

Siobhan: I have an aspirin! I always like to keep a packet in my handbag. For emergencies.

G/G: Here. Window. (*Leading Roderick to French windows*) (*To Siobhan*) Door.

Siobhan: Sorry?

G/G: It is day.

Roderick: The door, Siobhan. Just do it (*Siobhan stands by the door and G/G draws back the curtains*).

G/G: Now. Hands (*Inspects Roderick's hands*).

Roderick: Ouch!

G/G: Yes, yes.

Roderick: What is it? They are broken, aren't they?

G/G: No fracture. (*Patting Roderick's hands firmly*).

Roderick: Ow! No thanks to you.

G/G: Considerable contusion. (*Drawing the curtains meticulously shut*) First, leeches.

Roderick: What?

G/G: Reduce the swelling... Poultice, too. From forest flowers. Digit-alis.

Roderick: Digitalis?

G/G: Digitalis.

Siobhan: Excuse me, Mr...

G/G: Gunther-Gunther, manservant to Count Dracula. Door.

Siobhan: Oh, thanks. Is he, Mr Dracula... y'know, a vampire? The Count?

G/G: And cruel. *(Disappointedly)* Once.

Roderick: Nice touch, but vampires do not exist.

G/G: Wager your life against it?

Siobhan: No!

Roderick: There are no such things as vampires.

G/G: The Master. Undead.

Siobhan: Oh!

Roderick: He's trying to scare you.

Siobhan: I'm scared!

G/G: *(To Roderick)* Leeches grow leaner in your absence.

Siobhan: What about me?

G/G: *(Indicating the curtains)* Do not touch. The Count... Arrive shortly.

Siobhan: I'll go with you.

Roderick: Stay here. Be sociable.

Siobhan: He's a vampire!

G/G: Hundreds of years.

Roderick: Stay here. There are no such things as actual, living vampires.

G/G: Undead, yes. Thousands.

Siobhan: I'm definitely coming with you.

Roderick: No.

Siobhan: Please. I'll hold your hand. (*Pause*) Sorry. Look, Mr Peters...

Roderick: Roderick.

Siobhan: Roderick...

Roderick: No! We'll only be a few minutes. (*To G/G*) Let's see the taxman.

(*Gunther-Gunther leaves*)

Roderick: And Siobhan? 'Roderick', remember, while we're here? Fiancé, remember?

(*Roderick leaves*)

Siobhan: Yes, Roderick. But never at the office, Mr Peters.

(*Siobhan examines the bookcase and then throws herself onto the settee. She then rises and draws back the curtains, standing in the full sunlight and feeling rather pleased with herself. Suddenly guilty, she draws them shut again*)

Siobhan: (*Addressing the portrait above the fireplace*) Oh! So you're Mister Dracula? My name's Siobhan and I'm not scared. (*Pause, turning downstage*) Hello, Siobhan Bibelot... French? Yes, yes it is, for Trinket... (*Tired laughter*) you're not the first to say so, and... DON'T COME NEAR ME! No, that's not right...

(*The Count enters unnoticed by Siobhan*)

Siobhan: Oh, Hi! Yep, that's me, Siobhan, and I'm not scared of vampires.

Count: I am glad to hear it.

Siobhan: (*A sharp scream*).

Count: Sorry, I startled you.

Siobhan: Hello. It's nothing, really. You just scared me half to death (*looking the Count up and down with admiration*) but I don't mind…

Count: Marvellous! After all, it is why we are here.

Siobhan: Is it?

Count: Most certainly! I'd hate to have any of my guests leave on Monday without their being terrified at least once.

Siobhan: "My guests?"

Count: Forgive me. (*Bows in Prussian style*) I am Count Vladimir Imre Nicolai Dracula. I live here.

Siobhan: You're Count Dracula?

Count: In body, if not in soul. (*Laughs. No response from Siobhan*) It's a joke we vampires like to tell.

Siobhan: Oh.

Count: The undead, you see. We don't have souls. It's all part of not throwing reflections in mirrors, and that sort of thing. Shaving is a nightmare, you know. I've had my nose re-built a dozen times. Ha, ha! (*Laughs. No response from Siobhan*) Still, we vampires were never renowned for our sense of mirth. Too parochial, I suppose. (*Pause*) Is my tie straight?

Siobhan: It looks nice.

Count: (*Pleased*) Do you think so? I do so like to be noticed.

Siobhan: I was expecting someone more…

Count: Vampire-like?

Siobhan: And you're so…

Count: Un-vampire-like.

Siobhan: Handsome.

Count: (*Beaming*) Why thank you, although not wholly unexpected. Damn! I must stop saying that. 'Wholly' - sounds much too much like, um (*wincing*), 'Holy' (*Shudders*) as in 'Church'. Certain words, you see, and symbols antagonise we vampires. Avoidance of aforesaid is the key to our longevity. (*Pause*) Your pardon. Siobhan, if I heard correctly? (*Taking Siobhan's hand he bows towards it, not actually kissing it with his lips*).

Siobhan: Um, yep. That's me.

Count: A captivating name. You are like the crescent moon rising on a starlit winter's night, Siobhan. Your cusped beauty illuminates us all…

Siobhan: Oh, gosh.

Count: And yet, do I discern a mystery hiding within the shadow cast across its face? Can this be true?

Siobhan: (*Siobhan gives a momentary pause*) Me? Oh No. No secrets with me. My boss says he can read me like a headline.

Count: How enviably perceptive.

Siobhan: He's with Mr Gunther.

Count: Plain Gunther-Gunther will do, hyphenated. (*Pause*) Who is?

Siobhan: My boss. My friend, really, Roderick Peters. We're engaged, sort of. He was silly'ing around, and Gunther-Gunther opened the door and bashed him.

Count: Is he hurt?

Siobhan: No. Mr Gunther said he'd suck the swelling out with leeches.

Count: Blood? Perhaps I should… But, no.

Siobhan: He deserves it. He tried to scare me.

Count: Do you frighten easily?

Siobhan: Not me. I could stay a month and not be scared one bit. But Mr Peters… Roderick, he wanted to go home he was so frightened. But I made him stay.

Count: That's the spirit.

Siobhan: You know, *(Appraising him favourably)* you don't look like a vampire, Mr Dracula.

Count: Count, please.

Siobhan: *(Uncertainly)* One, two, three…

Count: *(Laughs)* Very good. Very sharp. Humour, how nice. I have a feeling that you and I are going to get on like a heretic on fire.

Siobhan: That's nice.

Count: Isn't it just? You see, I do so want to cultivate a sense of humour. Mortals, I feel, could grow to like us if we brought a smile to their faces, and not a whimper to their throats. People have come to regard us as killjoys.

Siobhan: Never! You're ever so funny, I bet.

Count: Well, yes, I could be.

Siobhan: And they just die laughing whenever you're about.

Count: Certainly, the succulent creatures died. But, oddly, never through an excess of glee. One supposes that generally they were frozen with terror, and not the least bit interested in parody. Or even double-entendres. The thought that they may soon become lunch made them dry up, as indeed… being lunch did.

Siobhan: They're my favourite; (*Mispronouncing*) double-entendrays.

Count: Quite delightful! I do so like a small joke.

Siobhan: Small ones tickle. Are you sure you're a vampire?

Count: I swear it on my own grave.

Siobhan: Roderick, Mr Peters, doesn't believe in any such things.

Count: A sceptic? He'll not be my first.

Siobhan: He wasn't mine, either. But Mr Dracula, you don't dress like a vampire either.

Count: Thank you! It's my new suit, is it not? I haven't seen anything this sharp since Van Helsing waved a wooden stake beneath my nose.

Siobhan: You look super.

Count: Don't I just? You see, sharp teeth and pale make-up is yesterday's ghoul. I'm a renaissance vampire. A modern Nosferatu with designer-labels and an eco-coffin.

Siobhan: Eco is ever so chick (*sic*) now. It's so on trend.

Count: I'm so glad. You see, living in Transylvania one can never be sure what is en vogue and what is dated. Living in (***insert name of suitable 'local' but remote town***) must be much the same.

Siobhan: Mr Peters will never believe you're a vampire.

Count: C'est la vie, as we cosmopolitan types say.

(*Roderick enters, backing through the door, each index finger bandaged to the middle finger of each hand*)

Roderick: They're not broken, no thanks to that oaf. He really has got leeches down there… (*looks up*) Oh, hi. (*To Siobhan*) I opted for the iced-water, instead.

Siobhan: Um, Roderick, this here is Count Vladimir… something-something Dracula. He lives here.

Count: I'm sorry to learn of your unfortunate-

Roderick: You're Count Dracula?

Count: (*Bows*) I am.

Roderick: You don't look like someone who drinks blood just for the Hell of it.

Count: Should I?

Roderick: Excuse me, but I came here – and it cost me plenty – expecting not a real vampire, but at least one that was plausible.

Count: Appearances can be deceptive.

Roderick: What happened to black capes and pointed fangs?

Count: I was just remarking to your dear fiancée how it is with we vampires in these modern times.

Roderick: And how is it with "we vampires"?

Count: Well, obviously the cape-thing is out. These days, I wouldn't be seen undead in one.

Roderick: Really?

Count: Absolutely! It is so passé. And take the expression, 'Vampire', for example? So vulnerable to accusation. I much prefer to identify as a 'Haemivore'. It is a better term for those who still practise.

Roderick: "Haemivore"?

Count: Oh, yes. For those who still practise. Personally, I've put behind me all those nights of flitting from virgin to virgin in search of a bite to eat. In its place has come diurnality - so long as the curtains are drawn - and a healthy diet.

Roderick: So it's forget the jugular puncture, and pass another bowl of muesli?

Siobhan: You're a vegetarian?

Count: And proud to be so.

Roderick: Bloody marvellous.

Count: Just "marvellous" will suffice.

Siobhan: I'm a veggie, too!

Count: I knew it! Do you like pulses?

Siobhan: Only when they're racing.

Roderick: Hold on. You don't look like a vampire and you don't eat what a vampire eats.

Count: Precisely. Do you want that I should arrange for a refund?

Roderick: Yes, perhaps you should.

Siobhan: Oh, let's stay! Please?

Roderick: So, Paris has lost its shine?

Siobhan: Paris could be fun, but here—

Roderick: No.

Siobhan: Oh, please! (*Moving close*) Hmmmm? Please?

Roderick: I should say "no" more often.

Siobhan: Me too.

Roderick: (*To the Count*) OK, we're staying, but I expect things to improve for tonight's Impaler's Banquet.

Count: Rest assured, Roderick, you will adore it. All the wine you can drink, all the food you can catch- Eat! Did I say "catch"? Oh, dear. A slip of the, um, tongue. Roderick, I promise you'll not be disappointed.

Siobhan: *(To Roderick)* I'll go with that.

Roderick: Well, at least the castle looks real enough.

Count: Oh, indeed. Completed by my father during the winter of 1398. Of course, I was just a small boy in those days, and Gunther-Gunther wasn't much older himself.

Roderick: That's better.

Count: Roderick, I am being perfectly honest.

Roderick: Good. Stay honest and tell us what an ex-vampire does in his spare time, now that you're not dining out every night.

Count: I have a gym, and a rigorous fitness regime. I like to keep myself nicely groomed, although the result is somewhat tarnished by my not being able to see myself in the mirror. I am forced to rely on Gunther-Gunther's uneducated and, I suspect, disinterested opinions. Between you and I, he doesn't know the difference between catwalk and cat litter.

Roderick: I'd never have guessed. Nice suit.

Count: It is, isn't it? Just a little something I chose from the catalogue. Ideally, of course, I'd purchase my clothes from a gentleman's outfitters - if they stayed open after sunset. But, tell me, who wants to be visited by a vampire after nightfall? Hmmm? And, um, your pastime? Roderick?

Roderick: Cubbing.

Count: Cubbing?

Siobhan: Fox-hunting.

Roderick: … But for the little ones.

Count: Oh, Roderick.

Roderick: It's fun! It's more horrific than this is.

Count: Those poor, fluffy—

Roderick: You're supposed to be a vampire, for Chrissake!

Count: Ouch!

Roderick: (*Oblivious*) I also import tropical fauna, finches being my particular speciality.

Count: Roderick, no. Not squashed into over-crowded cages, please.

Roderick: No! Of course not.

Count: Oh good.

Roderick: Toilet roll centres are my preferred method. Take an elastic band and PING! stop their tiny, delicate wings from flapping then, pop, into the tube. Three or four distributed throughout the pockets of my overcoat, and it's all too easy. Never been stopped by a border patrol yet.

Count: Roderick - I may regret asking this - but, um, what is it precisely that you do for a living.

Roderick: I'm in business.

Count: Any particular type of business?

Roderick: Mining - iron ore. And chemicals - pesticides.

Siobhan: And toxic waste. His acCountants say he's in it over his head.

Count: How very suffocating.

Roderick: The way I view toxic waste is that we, the resource rich countries, have all these by-products and the rest of the world have all the space.

Siobhan: The rest is business.

Roderick: Household product live-tissue trials. I like the phrase, Clinically Tested, don't you? So very reassuring.

Siobhan: Drift-net manufacture.

Roderick: Tobacco used to be good, before all the do-gooders, but I can still sell it in some places.

Siobhan: He has diverse interests, don't you, Mr Peters? - Roderick.

Count: So it would seem. Roderick, I can't help but feel that there is a certain - and please do not feel that I am implying any amount of criticism - a certain detrimental aspect to these ventures.

Roderick: You should see my bank account.

Siobhan: It's huge.

Roderick: And besides, if not me, then who? Someone has to do it.

Siobhan: And Roderick does it very well.

Roderick: Why thank you, darling.

Count: I expect this evening's banquet-table conversation to be most entertaining.

(Curtains Close)

ACT I SCENE 2

SCENE – *The Sword Room: Later, same afternoon. The curtains are open, allowing sunlight to flood the room.*

Gunther-Gunther enters, followed by Rebekah and Clemency.

G/G: The Sword Room. Here.

Rebekah: This is where the Spawn of Satan lives.

G/G: You refer to my Master, Count Dracula.

Rebekah: Only God knows how many poor maidens have met their doom within these iniquitous walls.

G/G: None, in recent past. (*Sadly*) None.

Clemency: (*Inquisitive; looking through the windows, picking swords from the walls, crossing to the fireplace to look at the objets d'art on mantelpiece*) Been saving his appetite, has he?

G/G: Humour? (*Following behind replacing all she touches*).

Clemency: Uh, kind of.

G/G: Suspect the Count will like you. Here, shortly.

(*G/G crosses to the curtains and meticulously draws them shut*)

Clemency: Leave them open, Gunth.

Rebekah: Like all vampires, our host shuns the Lord's good light of day.

Clemency: He's still holed up in his coffin? That man is lazy.

G/G: Count… Explain. Soon.

(**In the near distance, a wolf howls**)

Clemency: And will he explain that, too?

G/G: A wolf.

Clemency: I didn't think it was a virgin.

G/G: *(With relish in his voice)* Wolves... Why your driver brooked no delay on departure from the village. Why he flogs horses until they foam. Wolves. They pad the road in packs after dusk and can bring down a pair of matched stallions, leaving nothing whatsoever alive. Neither beast, nor driver, nor passengers.

Clemency: Hungry little devils.

G/G: Yes.

Rebekah: And they do the Count's bidding, the wolves?

G/G: Each of us. The Count's bidding. A prince amongst vampires.

Clemency: And are there many?

G/G: Princes?

Clemency: Humour?

G/G: *(Confused)* Madam?

Rebekah: Thousands, perhaps tens of thousands. Each one an abomination.

Clemency: You'd know, Rebekah. *(To G/G)* We travelled together for 300 miles on the same train, through some of the most spectacular scenery in Europe, and never passed a word. And do you know what? In the three hours we spent in that damn' wagon I learnt more about Transylvanian history and culture than I ever cared for.

G/G: *(To Rebekah)* Enjoy my Master's company. He has knowledge of local folk-lore.

Clemency: He should do, he's part of it. And what about this? *(Pulling a small cross from beneath her blouse)* Is this part of the local folk-lore, too?

G/G: (*Snarls*) Away!

Clemency: Doesn't it match my earrings?

G/G: Away! Or to me. The Count does not tolerate such symbolism. It is… unsettling. Provocative, even.

Clemency: Why all the fuss? Some old lady from the village gave it to me as I stepped from the train. I wanted to pay, believe me, but she wouldn't have it. She kept on pressing it into my hand.

G/G: She had no cause to do so. A fool. Superstitious locals.

Clemency: It's only a little cross.

G/G: Even so… Never wise to cross a vampire. (*Extending his hand*) Here… Safe care.

Clemency: Well…

G/G: Insist.

Clemency: If that's how you feel about it (*Moves to undo the chain about her neck*).

Rebekah: Miss Hoyden, no! Wear it all times. At all times.

Clemency: What for? Oh, come on, Rebekah. You don't honestly believe this tiny thing will protect me from a vampire, do you? And who believes in vampires, anyway?

Rebekah: The righteous believe. Do you deny the existence of God?

Clemency: There's a God, hence there's a Devil, right? And what's more devilish than a vampire? Quad erat "Demon"-Strandum, is that what you're telling me?

Rebekah: Mockery is no defence against the Legions of Evil. Satan's bondsmen are eternally among us, in both obvious and subtle disguises.

Clemency: Oh Rebekah, lighten up. There is no such thing as a vampire.

G/G: My master will arrive shortly. Decide for yourself.

Rebekah: Miss Hoyden, keep the cross about your person, I beg you.

G/G: (*Extending his hand, once more*) To me.

Clemency: (*Looking at Gunther-Gunther and tucking the cross back into her blouse*) A girl can't be too careful, anyhow.

Rebekah: The Lord's protection is manifest in that simple icon.

Clemency: (*Patting the now concealed cross*) This little thing? Just goes to prove that size isn't everything. Look, Gunth, I don't want to appear rude, but it's been a long day and I need to freshen-up. If your Count isn't here in 30 seconds flat then, I'm sorry, but I'm out of here and going for a shower… or maybe a swim in the moat, (*The Count enters unseen behind Clemency. G/G bows deeply*) and I'm staying there until I grow gills.

Count: Growing gills? I find wings so much easier.

Clemency: You're an angel?

Count: (*Laughs*) Delightful! Um, not exactly, no. Allow me to introduce myself; Count Vladimir Imre Nicolai Dracula. At your service (*Bows in Prussian style*).

Clemency: You're Count Dracula?

Count: In body, if not… The very same.

Clemency: *The* Count Dracula?

Count: You are much impressed, I can tell.

Clemency: You don't much look like a vampire.

Count: (*Sighs*) So I'm beginning to understand. Still, with two more guests yet to arrive, (*to Rebekah*) one can only hope.

G/G: Mrs Douay.

Count: *(Extending his hand)* I'm pleased to meet you, Mrs Douay.

Rebekah: *(Not taking his hand)* Rebekah. R.E.B.E.K.A.H.

Count: How very biblical. Rebekah. Mother to those fractious brothers Esau and Jacob, if my memory serves me well?

Rebekah: A vampire who reads the Scriptures?

Count: Know thine enemy.

G/G: And this… Miss Hoyden.

Count: *(Bowing as he did to Siobhan in Act I Sc 1)* I am understandably enchanted, Miss Hoyden.

Clemency: Yeah? Thanks. Call me Clemency. Clem, if you like.

Count: Clemency? You are blessed with a beautiful name, Miss Hoyden, and I am most pleased to make your acquaintance.

Clemency: You're after something.

Count: Your heart, perhaps?

Rebekah: Your soul.

Clemency: Just my luck. Sweet talk and sour intentions.

G/G: Miss Hoyden is from America.

Clemency: That's A.M.E.R.I.C.A. Mother to Democracy. But currently residing in London.

Count: It matters not. You are the first person from the New World that Gunther-Gunther has ever met *(G/G bares his teeth in a manic grin)*, and he's terribly excited.

Clemency: I bet he's a real party animal when he lets his hair down.

Count: Between you and I, he can be an animal, certainly, but only when the moon is at its fullest.

Clemency: Sure. In the meantime, I'm humming like the subway in rush-hour. I need to freshen-up.

Rebekah: I have never met a Christian who didn't smell nice. Am I right, Miss Hoyden?

Clemency: Rebekah's hot on matters spiritual. She's my un-adopted soul-sister.

Count: Pity I, who have never had a soul-mate.

Rebekah: Or a soul?

Clemency: *(To the Count)* Take my word for it, they're a pain in the neck.

Count: The nicest people are.

Clemency: And if I don't freshen-up, mine is going to leave me in disgust.

Count: In such circumstances we will detain you no longer and, Miss Hoyden, I would be honoured to escort you to your room.

Clemency: My, you're the audacious one.

Count: *(To Rebekah)* 7:30 for cocktails, Mrs Douay?

Rebekah: I look forward to our next en*Count*er.

Count: As do I. Adieu!

Clemency: *(As they exit)* Vlad the Impaler, huh? And just whom do you impale? And more importantly, with what?

(Clemency leaves, followed by the Count)

G/G: *(To Rebekah)* I have duties.

Rebekah: Gunther-Gunther, we must talk.

G/G: I? Poor company, Madam. Master and I long ago exhausted conversation.

Rebekah: It's not discourse that I seek, but answers. Gunther-Gunther, how long have you been in the Count's service?

G/G: Six hundred years.

Rebekah: Then he *is* a vampire?

G/G: You've seen him with your own eyes.

Rebekah: I want the truth, Gunther-Gunther. Is that man the Count Dracula? *The* Count Dracula, Dark Satan's Captain?

G/G: With your own eyes.

Rebekah: Tell me!

G/G: You're here to kill.

Rebekah: Not to kill! No. To destroy. Do you understand? For pity's sake, you must!

G/G: Ah, Madam. Completely. "Thou shalt not kill."

Rebekah: And yet, "Suffer not a witch to live."

G/G: Then you are shackled, madam, by your Bible. If the Count is a vampire, you must destroy him. But if he is a fraud, an entrepreneur, and you kill him, then you are breaking one of your tiresome Commandments. And it is upon my word as to whether you proceed.

Rebekah: Do not taunt me! If I do not strike, and he infects others with his evil, then I will have failed. Worse, through my own quiescence I'll have become an accomplice. The burden of such sin! But if I strike, and kill a man, a mortal being, I'm damned to Hell like any wretched villain.

G/G: If only Moses had brought down from the mountain an Eleventh Commandment, "Thou shalt sin and be forgiven, if only you intended well."

Rebekah: Fine! I'll choose my own fate.

G/G: Did I say that I would not help you?

Rebekah: You'll do it then; you'll tell me the truth?

G/G: Perhaps. Six hundred years is a long time in which to grow loyal, Madam. Six hundred years is also a long time in which to grow weary.

Rebekah: If it's redemption you're after—

G/G: No. Not that. Repentance and Heaven is not for me. Six hundred years of living and yet not living. Sustained by the Count, feeding off his evil. Six hundred years. I am weary of it. No, Rebekah Douay, when the last vampire is gone from within these walls I'll wither and I'll die. Nothing. Oblivion.

Rebekah: You will help me?

G/G: As I said, perhaps.

Rebekah: Bless you, Gunther-Gunther.

G/G: Let me dwell on it.

(The Count enters)

Count: Ah, there you are Gunther-Gunther. You were not in your quarters.

Rebekah: My fault. I asked him to stay.

Count: For any particular reason?

Rebekah: Small talk.

Count: Idle chatter? I am surprised. He and I long ago exhausted our conversational repertoire.

Rebekah: *(Pause)* We had an interesting discussion.

Count: You are fortunate, indeed. And now, if you will pardon us, there are details concerning tonight's banquet…

Rebekah: I was just leaving.

Count: Adieu, once more. *(Stopping Rebekah as she reaches the `door)* Mrs Douay? You are not travelling with your husband.

Rebekah: No. Jack rests with the Lord God.

Count: Your pardon, I was insensitive.

Rebekah: He was beautiful, Count, and one day I will go to him. He waits for me, I am without doubt.

(Rebekah exits. The Count rolls his eyes and crosses to the fireside chair, slouching in it)

Count: What have we learnt about our Mrs Douay?

G/G: Not all as it appears.

Count: There's more to her than the fiery zealot?

G/G: Suffer not a witch to live.

Count: Hardly a revelation, but thank you. And when am I to receive my retribution?

G/G: Tomorrow. Suspect.

Count: Can't you be more precise?

G/G: When is… convenient?

Count: Ah, I see. Thank you, Gunther-Gunther. *(Rising from chair)* We shall spin a web to catch this avenging wasp, and the threads will be like my hunger. Thank you, my friend.

(Gunther holds door open for Count. Count Exits. Gunther-Gunther switches main lights off. Black Out) (Curtains drawn back on French windows. Gunther-Gunther exits)

(Pause) (Debbie enters through French doors, shines phone torch around)

Debbie: We're definitely in the right place, Google maps said we've arrived at our destination.

(Kevin backs through doors, bumping into Debbie, startling them both. Debbie squeaks and slaps him)

Debbie: Don't!

Kevin: Oops, sorry.

Debbie: (*shines light around*) Where is everyone?

Kevin: Maybe a vampire got them!

Debbie: Maybe! Isn't this great!?

Kevin: SO great! I'm so scared my left arm is tingly!

Debbie: (*shines light under chin*) Do you think you'll have a heart attack?

Kevin: (*shines his light under chin*) Maybe!

Debbie: Ooh then I'll be left alone in this spooky castle with only your corpse for company… If you DO die, promise you'll haunt me?

Kevin: (*Walks around room, shining light here and there*) Technically, you're the oldest, so chances are you're going first.

Debbie: Okay then, if I die first I promise to haunt y—

Kevin: (*Finds door*) Oh! A door!

Debbie: OOOH!! Let's go!!!

(They run through, squealing excitedly)

(Curtains Close)

ACT 1 SCENE 3

SCENE – *The Sword Room: The room is lit by a single dim table lamp.*

Gunther-Gunther enters through the secret door and crosses to the window. He draws open the curtains. **Silvery moonlight** *falls into the room. He pauses, surveying the countryside beyond the castle.* **A wolf howls. An owl hoots.**

G/G: (*Looking at the moon*) A hunters' moon. Does anyone hunt this night?

(G/G crosses to the main door, switches on the main lights and exits through the secret door, ensuring it is closed. **The owl hoots** *once more as Clemency enters followed by Roderick, his knuckles covered in a smaller plaster)*

Rod: Look, I'm in touch with what needs to be done.

Clemency: No, Rod, you're out of touch. More than that, you're irresponsible.

Roderick: In your opinion. I'm a businessman, I employ eighty-six people in one factory alone. OK, fifty-four. I streamlined that company last week, but I'm a Nett Exporter.

Clemency: A Drift Net exporter.

Roderick: What I achieve is good for my nation and the government know it. Dig it up - catch it - kill it - ship it out - it's all good.

Clemency: How can it be good for any country when it's bad for the whole world? We only have one environment.

Roderick: Ugh, I hate the word, *environment*. Do you want to know why I hate it? Because in twenty years from now, it'll be out of date. No one will use it. Environment is a transient word, like "Tiktok" and "gender-fluid".

Clemency: Or asshole?

Roderick: What is wrong with extracting the carbon dioxide from old power stations?

Clemency: Nothing, it's a great idea. But do you have to export the gas to developing nations?

Roderick: Yes! No one else is gonna take it, are they?

Clemency: And you do all of this for the money?

Roderick: Of course. If it wasn't lucrative, I wouldn't do it.

Clemency: There! Condemned by your own words.

Roderick: Nonsense. If I didn't fill the niche someone else would.

Clemency: You cannot absolve yourself of responsibility by taking that argument.

Roderick: Who begs for absolution?

Clemency: You're destroying my world!

Roderick: Look, Clemency, these "green issues", they're just a fad. In the 1950s it was "invaders from Mars", in the 80's it was "Global Nuclear War" and now it's "Global Warming". There have always been doom-merchants - it's lucrative, by the way. Twenty years from now, they'll be railing against another "Population Explosion".

Clemency: There won't be a population if we don't act soon. There are villages not 200 miles from here where the average life expectancy is ten-to-fifteen years less than it is for you and I, and all due to pollution.

Roderick: And who lives there? I'll tell you; Not me.

Clemency: You bastard. Don't you care about what is happening to the rest of the world?

Roderick: Why should I? How can I get excited about the annihilation of a forest on the other side of the planet? It's far enough away not to intrude on my conscience.

Clemency: Get excited, Rod, you should get excited.

Roderick: Why?

Clemency: Because, sooner or later, its loss will cease to be your gain.

Roderick: Don't be fatuous. Listen, if there's a sewer outlet next to a beach, I don't swim there. I don't swim where there are turds and I don't mess on my own doorstep, understand?

Clemency: So where will you go when every beach stinks like a latrine?

(The Count enters with Siobhan)

Count: Do I hear the sound of duelling?

Clemency: To the death.

Roderick: All I'm saying is that it's not my problem.

Clemency: It's a problem that concerns everyone. The Count, Siobhan, that Roderick Peters fathead, myself.

Roderick: You err by twenty-five percent.

Clemency: Roderick! We are the pivotal generation.

Roderick: Listen, if I have desk in my office made from the finest Amazonian hardwood—

Siobhan: *(Snuggling ever closer to the Count)* Which he does.

Roderick: *(Gives Siobhan a sideways look before refocussing on Clemency)* Which I have, am I responsible for the destruction of the rainforest? No. It's just a little desk, and—

Siobhan: It's huge. Two people can lay on it flat-out naked without moving the telephone.

Roderick: And… I only bought it. If the desk wasn't for purchase it wouldn't be in my office right now. I didn't cut down the tree that made it. The wood came from someone else's garden.

Clemency: You make exploitation sound so glib.

Roderick: Where's the exploitation? The product was on sale. If I happen to drive a pre-catalytic converter classic car… (*Looking long and hard at Siobhan*) which I do, am I responsible for the alleged pollution? No. The same argument applies, and a little bit of nitrogen dioxide never hurt anyone. (*Pause*) That much.

Count: But Roderick, surely, if every person thought along those lines—

Roderick: So what? The world is a big place. It can carry a few bruises. Big noise. That's progress. What's wrong with processing seal pups into fashion accessories, and whales into cat food? What you lose in the environment, you gain in the chain stores.

Clemency: Stop it!

Siobhan: He doesn't use a product unless it's been tested on animals first.

Roderick: And proud of it. Tell me, has the disappearance of a hundred types of animal made the world a worse place? Again, no. And it wouldn't be any worse if all the tusks in Africa were carved into cutlery handles. That's right! Remember Dodos? Who misses them? Do you? In fact, the only good thing you could say about the Dodo is that their extinction coined a phrase, and led to the enrichment of the English language, so they, at least, have contributed something durable to our lives.

Clemency: You really are a rotten bastard.

Roderick: Wrong. Do you know who I am? I'm the man in the street. (*Eyeing Clemency who has taken her phone out of her pocket and is scrolling through it*) Not some plastic-hypocrite, rhyming the virtues of green-politics on a power-consuming plastic and silicon phone that they've upgraded 9 times since they were the same age.

(*Clemency surreptitiously puts her phone away*).

Count: (*Moving towards the drinks' table*) I think that now might be a suitable moment to pour the after-dinner drinks.

Clemency: Good idea. Venom over ice for my friend here.

(*Rebekah enters*)

Count: Ah, Rebekah, your timing is perfection itself. Care to join us in a glass of Werewolves' Blood?

Rebekah: I would not!

Count: No need to be alarmed. I've not seen the real thing since dear Aunt Melissa took a silver bullet in the chest. They buried her where she fell, on a hillside overlooking the village, with a wreath of wolfsbane about her neck. That night, a pack of timber wolves came down from the mountains, unearthed her shallow grave and ate her flesh, cracked her bones. (*Musing*) Dog eat dog, as they say.

Roderick: I love the sentiment.

Count: An individual liqueur (*Holding up a decanter of dark liquid*), distilled from the ferment of locally-grown paprika. The drink has a certain piquancy, ferocity some say, that I'm sure you find fascinating. The woodsmen hereabouts thrive on it and old hags use it to concoct strange cure-alls.

Roderick: I'll have one of those.

Count: Good for you, Roderick. It was very popular with my Uncle Yevgeny after his death in 1507. He swears by it.

Siobhan: Would you like to give me one?

Clemency: Count me in, Count. Maybe it'll take my mind off punching Rod.

Roderick: Punch away, I can carry a few bruises, too.

Count: You know, it's not often that I have the opportunity to take sides in an… um, discussion?

Clemency: Nice euphemism.

Count: Thank you. But in this case, I must say, Roderick, I share many of Clemency's perceptions.

Roderick: Count, I don't want to hear it. You're supposed to be a vampire, not an environmentalist.

Count: There's a great deal to be said for changing one's attitudes.

Clemency: And the change in you? Permanent, is it?

Count: Without doubt! And you admire the new me?

Siobhan: Oh, I do!

Clemency: It's passable. So, tell us what caused this image-boosting transformation.

Count: Oh no, I couldn't say so soon after dinner.

Siobhan: No, go on. Tell us.

Clemency: Listen to Siobhan.

Rebekah: Count?

Count: First, a little something to aid the digestion.

(Count serves the drinks to his guests in turn)

Count: Roderick?

Roderick: Of course. My compliments to the chef.

Count: *(To Clemency)* My dear?

Clemency: A little garlic wouldn't have gone amiss… still, in the circumstances.

Count: Siobhan?

Siobhan: Thank you.

Count: And for Rebekah, a glass of water from a pure forest stream.

Rebekah: You're very persuasive, Count.

Clemency: I bet all the girls used to say that.

Count: In truth, they seldom said anything.

Clemency: They just used to squeal a little, huh?

Count: Precisely! And for years that was the sum total of my conversation.

Siobhan: No vampire friends?

Count: Ever fewer and fewer, I'm afraid, and none abide locally, which is something of a blessing, (*looking at Rebekah*) if I may borrow the term, as their idea of gossip was to regurgitate an encounter with a particularly compliant and generous neck. I'm much happier since I gave up that sort of thing. Mortals are so interesting! There's more to a being, I've discovered, than just the six-inch strip of flesh between the jaw and clavicle.

Roderick: (*Measuring the distance with a span of his hand*) That's never six inches.

Siobhan: Oh yeah, six inches is average.

Clemency: Is that the sole reason you came off your liquid diet? Because it became a dull after-dinner topic?

Count: Not exactly, no, but such weariness, I feel, was a symptom of my burgeoning dissatisfaction with active vampirism. Here's to changing one's attitudes. (*Raising his glass*) A toast; to my delectable transformation... and to our pair of late arrivals. One hopes they have come to no harm.

Clemency: Why should they? You're staying in.

Count: Quite. Cheers!

All: Cheers!

(The Count unflinchingly takes a draught, as does Siobhan. Rebekah sips her water. Clemency and Roderick swig their drinks. Clemency catches her breath while Roderick explodes into a fit of coughing)

Roderick: Bloody hell! That stuff bites!

Clemency: Unlike our host, eh Count?

Count: Quite so. Another, Roderick? They say an excess of what you fancy does you good.

Roderick: Thanks, no!

Siobhan: *(Impatiently)* Well?

Count: Oh, yes. *(Clears his throat)* Let us see if I can give the tale some justice. *(Crosses to the window)* Imagine a moonless night in December. The wind dragging thick, heavy clouds across an impenetrable blanket of midnight black. **(The lights half-dim, leaving only the Count fully lit, bathed in moonlight)** A primeval hunger drives me from the castle walls in search of blood, and on the wings of a distant storm... **(The moonlight dims momentarily and a gentle rumble of thunder is heard)** comes the sound of thunder and scent of deluge. I fly swiftly, passing over several cottages before I arrive at a small dwelling on the outskirts of the village, the light from a single candle falling through the thin curtains of an upstairs room. I alight at this window, my leathery wings stretched wide, yellow eyes searching, and scratch at the pane with a sharp claw. Gently, seductively. At first only a silence greets this sound and I score the pane once more. Suddenly, a young woman of breath-taking beauty draws back the curtains.

Her hair is as black as the night sky and her eyes are endless wells of passion. She opens the window. "Enter," she whispers, before stepping back into the centre of the room. I glide in, and assume the shape of Dracula, Prince of Vampires.

(Room lights to full brightness)

Roderick: With a cape?

Count: With a cape.

Roderick: And slicked back hair, and sharp teeth?

Clemency: Shut up, Rod.

Count: I stand before her, staring compulsively into her wide eyes, as her hands move slowly, mechanically, to her throat and undo the buttons of her night-gown.

Roderick: Now you're talking.

Count: Moving close, I place my hands on her shoulders and ease the material away from her flawless skin. She sighs, softly, (*Siobhan and Rebekah who have been hanging on the Count's every word both sigh*) and my gaze slides from her eyes to her exposed neck. I bend forward my head, pause in delicious anticipation, and bite deeply into her yielding flesh.

Siobhan: (*Siobhan, who has been caressing her neck, stops*) Well?

Count: Blood poisoning. Riddled with it, I'm afraid. She looked like Hades but tasted like bile.

Clemency: I'm going to throw up.

Count: Did I not warn you? And, compounding my misery, the following night I chose the only diabetic in the village.

Roderick: For Chrissakes!

Count: Ouch!

Rebekah: Not for His sake, Mr Peters, not ever for His sake.

Count: My story is true, every word. That, of course, was the final nail in the coffin of my being a haemivore. I've been doing this for far too long, I thought. A fresh diet was desperately required and with it - miraculously - came a new life-style. A new Dracula.

Clemency: Brilliant, Count. You've almost convinced me you are the real thing. No fake could ever have dreamt up such an outrageous story.

Count: I'm believable because I'm so unbelievable?

Roderick: He claims to be six hundred years old, as well.

Clemency: Really? *(To the Count)* You must give me the name of your surgeon.

Count: A scourge on surgeons! One, many years ago, a vexatious and misguided fellow, by the name of Van Helsing—

Clemency: *(Looking at Rebekah)* The type who attempted to curb your appetite with a wooden spike and a fundamental enthusiasm?

Count: The very same.

Siobhan: But wasn't he… y'know, not real?

Count: Quite real enough to bleed, my dear, although Stoker understood him to be a product of my imagination.

Siobhan: Stoker? Stoker who?

Roderick: Bram Stoker, he wrote the novel, Dracula.

Count: Published in 1897.

Clemency: You knew Bram Stoker?

Count: I helped him to author the book. Cruden Bay, Scotland, during the wet summer of 1895.

Clemency: I love the angle; you're a figment of Stoker's genius, and yet you also helped him to write a book about yourself.

Roderick: A work of fiction. Which makes you…

Clemency: Clever. I like it. I bet old Van H. would have liked it too, (*sadly and with a trace of hurt*) had he lived.

Count: Sad to say, he didn't. Instead, I immortalised him in print.

Siobhan: Did he look like Hugh Jackman?

Count: The spit.

Clemency: Why didn't you let him go?

Count: That is where fact and fiction differ. Van Helsing wins, of course, in the novel. But in reality (*Pause*) self-defence. There was no reasoning with the man. Incorruptible, too.

Rebekah: Did he release many from their torment?

Count: They were my friends.

Rebekah: Do many remain?

Count: I am uncertain. Several hundred, perhaps, punctuate the face of the globe.

Rebekah: So few?

Count: We are not a prolific Sect, despite the folk-lore that would have it otherwise.

Roderick: But the bite of a vampire is contagious. If vampires existed. Which they don't.

Count: Such scepticism!

Rebekah: By such methods does Evil pollute the Innocent.

Count: If that were to be the case, Rebekah, do you not think that, by now, mortals would be up to their back teeth in vampires? Or should that be vice-versa? Do you not think that the undead would be swarming across all the continents in search of souls or, worse, be reduced to preying upon each other?

Siobhan: So how?

Count: Less than one percent of our *clients* become vampires. The rest simply died.

Siobhan: Which one percent?

Count: Why one person should wake after death and another not remains a lottery.

Rebekah: Your words are a revelation.

Count: And yours are poorly chosen, my dear. Yes, ignorance and superstition have plagued us - some of it at our own instigation, I will admit - for as long as I care to recall.

Siobhan: But it must have been nice being a vampire.

Count: The truth? Vampirism had its good points (*bares his teeth*), before losing its attraction. I'd call a Gathering, and thousands of vampires would congregate here, in my castle, on the longest night of the year. The mausoleum, the cellars, the dungeons would be choked with coffins, each one the not-quite-final resting place of a dear friend or relation. They were wonderful days. We'd sing, we'd dance, we'd invite a few local girls over for supper.

Siobhan: And that has all stopped?

Count: Oh, yes. I became dissatisfied with all the sordid bloodlust. Towards the end, I took no pleasure from being a hedonist. Add to that my encounter with the unsavoury brunette.

Clemency: And the no-doubt strident objections from many a local parent.

Count: Well, yes. Before long I'd lost several close companions to objectionable objectioneers. For myself, I was safe here, but many of my brothers and sisters were vulnerable, resting as they did in small plots across the old and new worlds.

Siobhan: Is that why there are so few of you left?

Count: I'm afraid so.

Clemency: Vampiral-prejudice. It's the same the world over.

Roderick: Listen, if vampires are such an endangered species, how come no-one has formed a protest group to save them?

Count: Roderick! What a fine idea!

Roderick: I wasn't being serious.

Clemency: I'll join! Vampirists will join ecological pirates as the new pariahs!

Rebekah: There are some who feel that such evil should be eradicated, and not preserved.

Siobhan: Mr Dracula's not evil, are you?

Count: Not so you'd notice, my dear.

Siobhan: So why don't you call another Gathering and explain how you feel to the other vampires?

Roderick: This is madness.

Clemency: You might even be able to form your own self-help group of veggie-vampires.

Siobhan: Then no-one could victimise you!

Count: You may have something. We could call ourselves "White Vampires" and help others who are less fortunate than ourselves.

Clemency: Or, "Green Vampires", with the accent on ecological issues.

Count: It may counter some of our adverse publicity.

Clemency: Why not become a blood donor?

Count: Wonderful!

Siobhan: What blood group are you?

Count: Do you know, I'm not sure? No-one has ever taken mine.

Roderick: This is becoming hard to swallow.

Clemency: Like the Werewolves' Blood?

Count: I've been struck by an idea! Many moons ago I hid an address book, incarcerated with Great Uncle Hector (*Nods to the portrait above the fireplace*) in the Moldavian Sepulchre. Tomorrow night, I shall exhume both Great Uncle Hector, who never liked the Moldavians, and the address book, and I shall write to every haemivore in it.

(Siobhan moves a step closer, looks seriously at the Count)

Rebekah: The Book exists?

Count: You've heard of it?

Clemency: Rebekah's done her research.

Rebekah: Is it current?

Count: Perhaps. We haemivores tend not wander once we have found a suitably inhospitable spot. (*Pause*) In fact, I shall go and fetch it now.

Clemency: Wait up, I'll come with you.

Rebekah: So shall I.

Siobhan: Me too.

Roderick: You'll stay here.

Clemency: Come on, Rebekah, give me a break.

Siobhan: Maybe she should go.

Rebekah: The Count is, by his own admission, the Prince of Darkness.

Clemency: He can have more titles than a shelf full of paperbacks, and I wouldn't be bothered one iota. Besides, I've got this (*She fishes the small cross from beneath her blouse*).

Count: Ugh! That horrid thing! Put it away!

Clemency: Sorry, I thought… (*Hastily, Clemency tucks the cross back into her blouse*).

Count: Perfectly alright, you weren't to know. Despite the passing of my old ways, I am still at the mercy of certain devices.

Clemency: I'll take it off.

Rebekah: No! Don't.

Count: Rebekah is right. There is no need to remove it from your person but, please, keep all such items out of sight. Besides, although unsettling, a little thing like that would never stop a determined vampire. It would take something much larger.

Rebekah: Like this? (*She pulls a fist-sized cross from her pocket*).

Count: (*Turning away*) Rebekah, please.

Clemency: Rebekah! What are you doing?

Rebekah: Prove yourself, Count. Are you a fraud or are you truly a vampire? Touch the cross. Save yourself.

Clemency: Rebekah! For Chrissake!

Count: (*Wails*).

Clemency: Sorry!

Rebekah: Well, Count?

Clemency: Leave him be!

Siobhan: (*Stepping between Rebekah and the Count*) He's hurting.

Rebekah: Of course he is. Look, a vampire!

Count: Take it away!

Roderick: (*To Rebekah*) There are no such creatures. He's just pretending, staying in character. And doing a damn' fine job.

Clemency: At last, Rod's said something sensible. (*To the Count*) You're good.

Roderick: It's why we're paying him.

Rebekah: Give him the cross. Ask him to return it to me.

Clemency: Let it go, Rebekah. You've made your point.

Rebekah: No. Let the Count prove to us, once and for all, that he's not a vampire. Take the cross from me and pass it to him.

Clemency: Count?

Count: I cannot.

Clemency: Oh, for God's sake.

Count: Don't make it worse.

Clemency: This has gone far enough. Give me that. (*Clemency snatches the cross from Rebekah*) Count, just take the cross and give it back to Rebekah.

Count: It's impossible.

Roderick: Count, we're living in the 21st Century. Vampires don't exist, if they ever did. Drop the pretence, we won't mind, just this once.

Clemency: Count! It sticks in my throat to say so, but Roderick is right. You're running a hotel, not a coven.

Count: I am sorry.

(The Count exits)

Clemency: Wait!

Rebekah: I have my answer.

Clemency: (*Throwing the cross underarm towards Rebekah*) You look after this for me, OK?

Rebekah: Take it with you! Your soul is in peril.

Clemency: When I get back, so is your ass.

(*Clemency leaves. A pause*)

Rebekah: Miss Hoyden doesn't realise the danger she is in.

Roderick: Nor do you, I think.

Rebekah: She won't accept my help.

Roderick: Rebekah, Clemency is big enough to get into trouble without your assistance.

Rebekah: I shall pray for Miss Hoyden.

Roderick: If I were you I'd save it for myself.

Rebekah: (*Placing the cross on the table*) This, I shall leave here. It has often been a source of great comfort.

Roderick: We shan't be needing it, thanks.

Rebekah: I shall pray for you all.

(*Rebekah leaves*)

Roderick: What a woman!

(*Roderick is talking about Rebekah – Siobhan is inferring Clemency*)

Siobhan: I don't like her all the same.

Roderick: She's not so bad. Over-zealous, perhaps.

Siobhan: She'll cause trouble, you wait and see.

Roderick: Maybe. Although the Count is capable of looking after himself. Probably.

Siobhan: Why can't she go home and leave us be?

Roderick: No refund, I guess.

Siobhan: And have you seen the way she looks at him? He's not safe.

Roderick: Do you think she'd actually?

Siobhan: Without so much as breaking into a sweat. Bitch!

Roderick: Hey! Come on.

Siobhan: Well, she is. *(Imitating Clemency)* "When I get back, so's your ass!"

Roderick: Clemency?

Siobhan: She's a right tart.

Roderick: She's allowed to be.

Siobhan: She sticks to his side like perspiration to the bottom sheet.

Roderick: You're jealous! You ought to remember whose girl you are.

Siobhan: I am not jealous! Honest. I just don't like her sort. I bet she can't lay on her back and press her knees together.

Roderick: Lucky him.

Siobhan: He deserves better than her kind.

Roderick: Will you shut up.

Siobhan: If that's what you want. *(Pause)* Do you think he really is a vampire?

Roderick: There are no such things. He's Counterfeit, believe me. If he isn't, we are in deep, deep trouble.

Siobhan: How come?

Roderick: What if he thinks he truly is Dracula? Hmmm? We could be sharing a weekend with a man who ought to be in an institution weaving baskets with Napoleon.

Siobhan: I think he is a vampire. A real one. A nice one.

Roderick: No, the idea is too fantastic.

Siobhan: But what if there are vampires, and ghosts, and poltergeists in this world? And witches, too. And people who make pacts with the Devil, and… well, anything. You don't know.

Roderick: I do. It is all utter nonsense.

Siobhan: But Rod, think of it. Vampires, who live forever. No growing old, no waiting for that first wrinkle. No wilting breasts, or slack thighs, or painful joints. No hair shot with grey. I want to puke when I see old women with their bloated ankles and feet stuffed into worn slippers. Ugh! I want none of it, Rod. None of it. No dentures, or failing eyesight, or asking younger people to speak up when I'm unaware that they're making fun of me. No forgetting my husband's name. No gravestone, Rod. Think of that.

Roderick: Siobhan, all the money in the world cannot change the fact that the gravestone is our sole reward. Myself included.

Siobhan: Not for him, it isn't. Not for the immortal Mr Dracula.

Roderick: (*Looking down, near Siobhan's feet. She is near the door*) What's that?

Siobhan: (*Stooping*) Somebody's jewellery?

Roderick: A cross. Not just any cross. This looks like the one Clemency was wearing.

Siobhan: How did it get here?

Roderick: The chain must have snapped. Wait. This is strange. The chain is intact.

Siobhan: And the clasp… it's still joined.

Roderick: As if she had lifted the chain over her head. This is hers?

Siobhan: Oh forget it. It could belong to anybody, and besides, she can look after herself. You said so. (*becoming seductive*) And… if you come with me… I'll look after you.

Roderick: She'll be OK?

Siobhan: Of course she will. Let me show you Paris.

(*Siobhan exits*)

Roderick: Yeah.

(*Pocketing the cross, Roderick exits. - A pause. G/G enters via the secret door, clears away the drinks that have been left, picks up the large cross from the table, studies it, and is about to leave by the same door when, the handle of the other door begins to turn. He conceals the cross on his person and quickly pushes the secret door shut. Rebekah enters*)

Rebekah: Gunther-Gunther.

G/G: Madam?

Rebekah: The cross… (*Noticing that it is missing*) I left a cross which should be with Miss Hoyden. She must keep it close at all times.

G/G: Hoyden? Peters took…

Rebekah: God be praised, and keep her safe. Gunther-Gunther, I know the course of action I must take.

G/G: Destruction.

Rebekah: Yes.

G/G: You would gamble with eternity?

Rebekah: Prayer has fortified my heart.

G/G: You are still willing to risk your soul?

Rebekah: For the book!

G/G: Containing the address of every known vampire.

Rebekah: Think of the glory!

G/G: Each vampire that still endures.

Rebekah: Praise be! I cannot forgo something so precious. The book must be ours.

G/G: We are set upon a path of irrevocable destiny.

Rebekah: Tonight, now.

G/G: My Master is strong while the night lingers.

Rebekah: I fear him not.

G/G: Defeat may bring you to the lap of your god, but it is victory that we seek.

Rebekah: Tomorrow, then, at dawn.

G/G: At midday. Powerless then.

Rebekah: We shall be revered, Gunther-Gunther. Revered.

(Rebekah exits)

G/G: *(Looking at the cross he has taken from his pocket, and moving to the secret door)* Saints are revered, Madam. But you and I?

(G/G leaves via the secret exit. A pause. The Count enters via the main door, blowing the dust from a small leather-bound book)

Count: My gratitude, *(nods to the portrait)* Uncle Hector, and with it my apologies for disturbing your sleep. Was there ever a more cantankerous skeleton? Still, if I had been interred with the Moldavians for 300 years.

(G/G re-enters via the secret door)

Count: Ah, Gunther-Gunther.

G/G: Master.

Count: Was there something? Information?

G/G: (*Sighs*)

Count: Well? Be quick.

G/G: Duplicity.

Count: Mrs Douay.

G/G: As I said before, Master, suffer not a witch to live.

Count: Most unsurprising.

G/G: One other.

Count: Is it so obvious that you need not enlighten me?

G/G: Hoyden…

Count: Stop! Gunther-Gunther.

G/G: Hoyden! (*Passing a woman's purse to the Count*) Here. Her room. Clemency Van Helsing.

Count: You're mistaken?

G/G: I am thorough.

Count: (*Leafing through a sheaf of credit cards, business cards, Driving licence, etc*) Why, Gunther-Gunther?

G/G: She is a maiden, like any other. A century ago you would have taken her blood and revelled in the taste of it.

Count: Yes, you are right. Once again, my friend you have been of immeasurable value.

Clemency: (*Off stage*) Count?

(*The Count passes the purse to G/G, who conceals it about his person. Clemency enters*)

Clemency: I'll be damned.

Count: Join the club.

Clemency: It's so beautiful in there. Spooky, but beautiful.

Count: Perhaps if you had caught Great Uncle Hector's outburst come here, my dear. (*Taking a cobweb from Clemency's hair*) Beautiful, but dusty. May I press upon you a night-cap and a mellow interlude of fire-side conversation?

Clemency: Damn, I love the way you speak.

Count: A Werewolves' Blood?

Clemency: (*Sitting in the leather chair*) Brandy. A small one. It brings out the worst in me.

Count: Myself included, which is why I shall be having a large measure. Gunther-Gunther, two brandies. (*G/G moves to the drinks' cabinet. As he prepares the drinks, Debbie backs through the main door, scolding Kevin in a loud whisper*)

Debbie: Put that down! We don't know where it's been!

(*Debbie turns to find the room is occupied. Kevin enters looking intensely at the taxidermy bat he is holding. Debbie puts an arm out to stop him. He drops the bat and they both stand like deer in headlights*)

Count: How inconvenient. It appears our late arrivals are here at last. Gunther-Gunther would you escort them directly to their room?

(*Debbie tries to discreetly retrieve the bat from the floor, noticed by Gunther-Gunther, who rebukes her with a firm, 'NO'. As she rises, Gunther-Gunther bends down and picks the bat up*)

G/G: Sir, madam, this way… (*Debbie and Kevin follow G/G out the door. The Count pours two brandies*)

Count: Have you made up your mind?

Clemency: About what?

Count: As to whether I am a vampire, or not?

Clemency: I don't much care either way. I think you're just fine. Whoever or whatever you are.

Count: You are very sweet *(Passing her a brandy glass).*

Clemency: Thanks *(Sipping her drink)* Mmm, so's that.

Count: Cheers?

Clemency: Sure, cheers. Here's to bringing out the worst in each other.

Count: *(Eying Clemency's neck)* I cannot think of a more appropriate toast.

(Clink of glasses – Black Out)

(Curtains Close)

(End Of Act I)

ACT II SCENE 1

SCENE – *The Sword Room: Daytime, Next Day. The curtains are shut against the sunlight.*

The Count is standing, both Kevin and his fresh-faced wife, Debbie, are sitting on the settee.

Count: You are not frightened easily, I imagine.

Kevin: Terrified at the slightest thing, actually.

Debbie: Me too, jump at my own shadow.

Count: How intriguing. And yet you've chosen to spend the weekend at a vampire's castle. You do realise this is a vampire's castle?

Kevin: Oh, yes.

Debbie: It's just as we imagined.

Kevin: More so, even.

Debbie: We couldn't have picked a better place.

Kevin: These Gothic fortresses are so supernatural.

Debbie: Atmospheric.

Kevin: Bats, belfries, things that go bump in the night.

Debbie: Everything about it makes me shudder.

Kevin: It's ever so scary.

Debbie: Ever so.

Count: One moment. Your capacity to withstand the fiendish seems to be as scant as I've ever encountered, and yet, here you are participants at Count Dracula's Horror Weekend. *(They nod vigorously)* I wonder why you're not in (**insert name of suitable local "sleepy" town**). I understand, (**insert name**) is very soothing at this time of year… or indeed, any time of year.

Debbie: Oh, no! We couldn't.

Kevin: You see, we like being terrified.

Debbie: Yes, we live for that scared to death feeling. Don't we, Kevin?

Kevin: Oh, yes.

Debbie: There's nothing quite like it.

Kevin: Do you have a dungeon?

Debbie: Ghosts?

Kevin: We adore haunted places. Debbie once saw an apparition in Edinburgh.

Count: They say it is not unusual.

Debbie: I was so scared.

Kevin: Absolutely petrified.

Debbie: *(Thrilled)*... I...

Count: Yes?

Kevin: Absolutely petrified.

Debbie: *(More thrilled)*... I...

Kevin: *(Stealing her thunder)* She wet herself.

Count: You must have felt very pleased.

Kevin: She has all the luck.

Debbie: I do! So does Kevin, sometimes. Remember the ouija board in Brittany?

Kevin: Brilliant! I was told—

Debbie: By someone of the Other Side.

Kevin: That's right, the Other Side, that I would become a victim of the Toilet Monster.

Count: Forgive me, the… er, the who?

Debbie: The Toilet Monster.

Kevin: The monster who lives in your toilet.

Count: And you have one, do you?

Debbie: Everybody does. It lurks in the littlest room…

Kevin: Sometimes on the landing…

Debbie: In the middle of the night.

Kevin: After everyone has gone to bed.

Debbie: And it waits, with infinite patience, for the unwary to wake up and go for a widdle at three in the morning.

Kevin: He's why most people lie awake for hours and hours…

Debbie: Crossing their legs…

Kevin: Kidding themselves it's not worth the effort to get out of bed.

Debbie: But really, they're scared in case the Toilet Monster eats them.

Kevin: After Brittany, I used to set the alarm every night for a whole month and go for a tinkle an hour after we'd snuggled beneath the blankets.

Debbie: He never used to switch the light on, either. The Toilet Monster only likes the dark.

Kevin: I'd be shaking like a leaf, too.

Count: A combination of factors that must have wrought merry havoc with your cork tiles.

Debbie: I used to bury my head under the pillow and wait for the screams.

Kevin: I was so terrified, that by the time I got to the bathroom I couldn't stop myself peeing even if I wanted to.

Debbie: Worst luck, he never saw it though.

Kevin: But once, I pretended I had, and screamed out really loud.

Count: And, um, Debbie?

Debbie: Yep, I wet myself.

Count: Remarkable.

Debbie: This is my treat to Kevin, for consolation.

Count: How splendid. Well, I'm afraid I can't promise you a Toilet Monster, but I know we do have a lost spirit in the north turret. I know, because I put him there. Ha, ha! What do you think of that?

Kevin: Can we go looking for him?

Debbie: I'll take a change of knickers.

Kevin: She always keeps a spare pair with her.

Count: How commendable. Yes, feel at liberty to roam wherever your inclination leads although, be warned, some of our cupboards do contain actual skeletons.

Debbie: Delicious.

Count: And what's more, if you are in anyway dissatisfied with your room we'll have you moved into the spare crypt, next to mine.

Kevin: Would you?

Count: No trouble at all. There are plenty of unoccupied vaults. Now, would you prefer a double sarcophagus, or a pair of singles?

Debbie: Singles, please.

Kevin: The isolation heightens our sense of fear.

Debbie: And are there rats?

Count: *(Disappointedly)* Hosts of them, I'm afraid.

Kevin: And do they run across your face when you're fast asleep?

Count: Only when I forget to close the lid after me.

Debbie: *(Thrilled)* Wonderful.

Kevin: We'd love to.

Count: I'll have Gunther-Gunther make up your caskets immediately.

(Roderick enters, two very small plasters across his knuckles)

Count: Ah, Roderick. Good morning.

Roderick: Don't I know it. Count I need to speak with you.

Count: Oh, dear, something not to your satisfaction?

Roderick: No complaints. This is business. Important business.

Count: Ah, the entrepreneurial spirit. I have one in the north turret.

Roderick: Pardon?

Count: That was humour. *(Uncertainly, to K & D)* Wasn't it? *(They nod)*.

Roderick: Was it?

(Siobhan enters)

Siobhan: Hello Mr Dracula!

Count: Good Morning, Siobhan. I trust you slept well?

Siobhan: Like one of the dead.

Count: How coincidental. Join us. We were just being humorous.

Siobhan: Oh, brill. I know a joke.

Roderick: *(To Siobhan)* Not now. *(To the Count)* Count, how long do you think it took us to drive here from the airport?

Count: I couldn't possibly guess. However, as the bat flies…

Roderick: Three hours. Three enlightening, lucrative hours.

Debbie: Through wolf-infested forests.

Siobhan: It's ever so funny.

Roderick: *(Ignoring Siobhan, and replying to Debbie)* Wonderful. Wolves and forests. My observations exactly. Wolves and forests.

Siobhan: I just remembered it. It's about vampires. *(To the Count)* You won't mind, will you?

Kevin: Did you see any, then?

Count: *(To Siobhan)* Not in the slightest.

Roderick: See what?

Siobhan: When my friend told me, I nearly wet myself.

Count: Perhaps Debbie might like to… um… ?

Debbie: We drove mostly at night, but we didn't see any.

Roderick: See any what, for Chrissake?

Count: Ouch! Roderick, that word.

Roderick: Sorry!

Kevin: Wolves!

Roderick: Wolves? No, we didn't either. As such, in the flesh. But that is not important. We all know they're out there.

Debbie: We like wolves.

Siobhan: I don't.

Count: The forest is thick with them.

Roderick: *(Looking at Kevin)* The thicker, the better. *(To the Count)* Now, if we can just focus on that fact for a moment? Wolves. Packs of them roaming the forest, out there.

Kevin: We have a little West Highland White Terrier at home.

Roderick: Really? And when did digression ever close a deal? Now then, Count - and Kevin was it?

Kevin: *(Sitting forward, trying to concentrate)* Was it what?

Roderick: *(Giving Kevin a confused frown before going back to the Count)* Anyway, wolves aren't just a voracious appetite on four paws, are they? Wolves, and other animals are—

Debbie: We call him, Akela.

Roderick: *(continuing)* –are a natural resource.

Count: *(to Debbie)* Who?

Roderick: *(To the Count)* The wolves. Animals.

Debbie: *(To the Count)* Our Westie! Like the wolfpack leader in *The Jungle Book*.

Roderick: And not just animals. The forest in its entirety as a composite product.

Count: Akela? He's not lupine, is he?

Debbie: Oh, no!

Kevin: He's very stable.

Roderick: As I see it, this whole region is underdeveloped.

Debbie: For a terrier.

Roderick: It's been neglected.

Debbie: *(Indignantly)* My mum's taking care of him.

Roderick: What?

Kevin: He's not neglected. Debbie's mum is looking after 'Kela until we get back.

Roderick: Akela? Forget your bloody dog! Count, do you realise the consequences of what I'm proposing? We have an opportunity, here, to bring un-thought of changes to this area. When I look out through the window (*moves towards the curtains*), what do I see?

Count: Roderick, no! Not the curtains.

Roderick: (*Impatient*) Hell.

Count: That is much nicer.

Roderick: OK, what would you say if I said that beyond your castle walls lies the salvation, in part, of the human race?

Siobhan: Can I tell my joke now?

Roderick: No!

Count: I'd say, how could that be?

Siobhan: The resources of today are the foundations of tomorrow. Isn't that right, Mr Peters? And please…?

Roderick: Once more! And you're for the sack.

Siobhan: You really know how to sweet-talk a girl.

Roderick: Not that sack. (*To the Count*) Siobhan's correct, even if speaking out of place.

Siobhan: It's what you said in Brazil.

Roderick: I know what I said in Brazil! Count, what I'm saying now is our modern society requires raw materials with which to perpetuate our civilisation, yes? Without a stock of fundamental components with which to produce the machinery of contemporary existence, subsequent generations will fall rapidly into anarchy. Thousands of years of progress will have been in vain.

Count: And how does this affect my wolves and forests?

Roderick: Three hours from the airport to here, and I didn't see a single factory. Not a strip-mine. Not one managed woodland. It's a wilderness out there, Count. No ski-slopes, no dams, no hotels. The area is criminally under-exploited.

Count: But, Roderick, it's beautiful.

Roderick: It's empty.

Siobhan: Please let me tell my joke. I'll forget it otherwise.

Roderick: Be quiet! (*To the Count*) We could start gently… with tourism, say. Tourism has potential even though the infrastructure can sometimes be expensive.

I was visualising along the lines of hunting lodges. What do you think? Go up-market. Fill the woods with well-heeled predators. Or! We could go for the straight cull. Do you realise how much a wolf pelt is worth when it passes through the right warehouse? Bear skins, too. We could corner the European trophy market. I hear Dollars and Euros, Count. Yen and Dinars.

Deer, elk, wild boar, hawks. Eggs. Wildflowers? Why not? Botany is business. Anything. Any damn thing that runs, crawls, flies, or grows. Clear the woods for the trees and then we begin logging. Simple.

Siobhan: Just like… what was the place in Asia? (*Pause*) It's funny, honest. My friend told it to me when I told her we were coming here.

Roderick: Logging! The world needs hardwoods, everyone else is stopping them being cut down and you have an abundance here. Then once the ground is clear - mining and then - am I a genius? Ten or twenty years from now, we can relocate toxic waste into the empty mines. Think of the benefits! Long-term income for the area. For you. And the eco warriors can't say anything if we keep it quiet. Everybody is happy. Us majorly.

Count: I think I should like to hear Siobhan's joke.

Siobhan: Thanks, Mr Dracula.

Count: We listen in good-natured anticipation, my dear.

Roderick: Count, forget Siobhan's pathetic joke. All that I am proposing is a natural progression, nothing more.

Siobhan: Ready?

Roderick: Animals. Trees. Minerals. Waste.

Siobhan: OK. (*Pause*) I used to be a vampire, but I'm alright nowwwwww!

Count: Very good. I think.

Debbie: Shouldn't it be a werewolf?

Siobhan: I used to be a vampire, but now I'm a werewolf?

Count: Oh, yes! I see. I was once a vampire, but now I am a werewolf. Most amusing.

Siobhan: Does that make sense?

Count: Quite.

Roderick: Count?

Siobhan: I'm not very good at remembering punchlines.

Count: You were wonderful.

Roderick: Count!

Count: Roderick?

Roderick: My proposition?

Count: Yes. If I understand you fully, your intention is to strip the land of its beauty, of its assets.

Roderick: And then some.

Count: To leave it barren?

Roderick: To bleed it dry, Count. Bleed it dry.

Count: Apparently we are both vampires.

Roderick: Thanks for the compliment. So, you're interested?

Count: No, I don't think so. Environmental leeching ill suits a compassionate nature.

Roderick: That is exactly the kind of wokeness I'd expect from Miss Hoyden.

Kevin: Who's Miss Hoyden?

Roderick: A late sleeper, I'd imagine.

Siobhan: *(Sarcastically)* Still in bed, is she?

Count: Um, not as such.

Siobhan: She looks like the type who has trouble getting off her back.

Count: She's gone. Departed, we think.

Debbie: Dearly departed?

Count: Oh, no. Nothing like that. This is somewhat embarrassing, but she appears to have… she's not in her room.

Roderick: So where is she?

Count: Neither Gunther-Gunther nor myself can say precisely where Clemency would be at this moment.

Roderick: But you can say where she isn't.

Count: Yes! Which is a source of some small reassurance, wouldn't you say?

Roderick: She's disappeared?

Count: Apparently so. *(Brief consternation from the others)* Gunther-Gunther made to rouse her this morning, for breakfast, and discovered the room empty.

Roderick: Her luggage?

Count: Unpacked and hanging neatly in her wardrobe.

Roderick: Why would she leave without taking her clothes?

Siobhan: Why not? She hardly wears any.

(Rebekah enters)

Rebekah: Good Morning. Count, you set a tempting table.

Count: Thank you. You know, I have always been capable of marked temptation, even as a child. My nanny could hardly keep her teeth to herself.

Rebekah: I dined simply.

Count: How beautifully pious.

Roderick: Shouldn't we be searching, instead of discussing—

Rebekah: Searching? For who?

Roderick: Clemency.

Rebekah: Miss Hoyden?

Siobhan: She's gone missing, worst luck.

Roderick: Her room's empty.

Debbie: Nobody knows where she is.

Kevin: Nobody, except…

(All look at the Count)

Count: Not true! Gunther-Gunther scours the castle even as we debate her absence.

Debbie: *(Excitedly)* You've killed her, haven't you?

Count: Debbie, please! Not even in jest.

Kevin: Bit her neck and sucked the warm life-blood from her veins.

Count: No!

Debbie: Did she call out?

Kevin: Did she scream?

Count: No! *(Pause)* I mean… I actually meant to say…

Debbie: Or was she compliant?

Count: Debbie, you are quite mistaken!

Rebekah: Count Dracula?

Count: I am innocent. Or as innocent as it is for a haemivore to be.

Rebekah: Where is Miss Van Helsing?

Siobhan / Kevin / Debbie / Roderick: Who?

Count: Ah for those who weren't aware, Miss Hoyden – Clemency, guested here under an assumed name.

Rebekah: You were aware?

Count: Yes. Clemency told me herself.

Debbie: She confessed! Under who-knows-what outrages?

Kevin: A vampire-hunter in Dracula's castle!

Debbie: No wonder she's vanished.

Count: Debbie! Miss V... Clemency has not vanished. She is merely... between appearances. She may have simply gone for a walk.

Siobhan: What did you two get up to last night?!

Count: If I were to say, a quiet drink, a cosy chat?

Rebekah: Did you kill her, Count?

Count: Positively not, Rebekah.

Siobhan: Cross your heart?

Count: Such a dreadful turn of phrase.

Rebekah: Liar! Oh, penance is mine!

Count: Rebekah!

Debbie: In the clutches of a vampire! When I die, that's how I want to go.

Count: *(Shouts, exacerbated)* Debbie!

Debbie: Oh! *(Debbie clinches her thighs together)*

Rebekah: Repent! Repent if you can.

Count: Please, everyone—

Rebekah: Beware, Dracula! I am a soldier of the Almighty!

Count: Rebekah! Discretion is such an admirable quality-

Rebekah: Guard yourself!

(Rebekah moves towards the door)

Count: —and one which really ought to prevail in the current circumstances.

Rebekah: When I return it will be with the means of your destruction!

(Rebekah exits, singing 'Onward Christian soldiers' off-stage, fading)

Count: Rebekah! Oh, hell!

Roderick: Why don't we organise a search party, and find the mysterious Miss Van Helsing before Rebekah returns? Count?

Count: Gunther-Gunther has a sixth-sense when it comes to finding women, believe me. You would only be getting in the way.

(G/G enters)

Count: Ah, Gunther-Gunther. Timely as ever.

G/G: Mrs Douay. Agitated. Assistance Master?

Count: There has been a misunderstanding.

Roderick: One which is about to be painfully compounded, should Rebekah return before we have found Miss Van Helsing.

Count: Oh, dear. *(To Gunther-Gunther)* Is any darkness to be thrown on her whereabouts?

G/G: None. This. *(Holding up a ladies dressing gown)* found outside. *(Indicating the blood-stained collar)* Blood. Found near castle wall.

Count: Miss Van Helsing's?

Roderick: That's a fair guess.

Count: This looks all, um, very conjecturable, doesn't it?

Roderick: You've articulated my thoughts, Count.

Count: Yes. *(Pause)* I do hope Clemency is fine. *(Pause)* You don't think…?

Debbie: I do!

Kevin: Me, too!

Count: Do I look like a vampire – Haemivore?

Roderick: Appearances can be deceptive. Isn't that what you said?

G/G: Leaving. Continue search.

Count: Yes. Well done.

Roderick: I'll help. Where did you find the gown?

Debbie: Can we search the dungeons?

Kevin: And the north turret?

G/G: If you wish.

Siobhan: Mr Peters, I'm scared.

Roderick: We're not leaving.

Count: There is no reason to, after all.

Roderick: Clemency can play hide-and-seek until she turns blue, for all I care. You and I are staying, at least until the Count and I have concluded our business. Count?

Siobhan: But what about her dressing gown? The blood… What if … (*Looks at the Count*) If…?

Count: Siobhan, I'm wounded.

Debbie: Not as wounded as you're going to be if Rebekah comes down and we haven't found this woman.

Kevin: She's going to stick you.

Count: I can empathise.

Debbie: What a way to go. A stake thrust through the heart!

Kevin: When it's my turn, that's how I want to go.

Debbie: Through the chest with it!

Count: Stop! Gunther-Gunther, would you please escort Kevin and his wife to the dungeons?

Kevin: Are you going to put us in chains?

Debbie: We wouldn't mind.

Count: It seems I still have a great deal to learn about temptation.

G/G: Search. Now.

Debbie: I hope there are loos down there.

G/G: Many years ago, the dungeons were used as a larder. My Master would keep sufficient nourishment down there to last several weeks.

Debbie: Their screams would become lost amongst the convoluted stone-lined passages.

Kevin: Never seeing daylight.

G/G: (*Exiting*) Yes. We'd feed them on a thrice-daily diet of spinach and liver, and at the end of a fortnight, why, they'd be bursting to see a vampire.

(G/G exits, followed by Kevin and Debbie)

Roderick: I'll search the stables.

Siobhan: Me too.

Roderick: No need. Stay here and stall Rebekah if she returns. Tell her not to do anything - anything - until I get back.

Siobhan: But...

Roderick: And don't let the Count of your sight. He and I have a deal to sign.

Count: Such persistence ought to be rewarded. I suspect that you are considered a formidable opponent, Roderick.

Roderick: You and I both. Kindred spirits. (*To Siobhan*) I'll be back in ten minutes. And relax, you're as safe as the Serengeti's only tuskless elephant. There's no such thing as vampires, remember?

(Roderick leaves)

Count: He's wrong, of course. About vampires, and not your well-being. (*Pause*) I have failed to convince you, have I not?

Siobhan: I like you, Mr Dracula, really I do. But Clemency. Are you really a vampire?

Count: Certainly. I have been all my life… and death.

Siobhan: There you go again! You say you're a vampire, but you don't look like one. You're really nice. Not like Roderick. We could all disappear and he wouldn't care one bit. He's only happy when he's wheeling and dealing. It's not like he needs the money. He has millions and millions anyway. He just likes ruining things, what with his palm oil businesses, his trawlers, timber companies, and mining companies. Oil. He doesn't make anything, except money. He takes and takes, and he takes. You, you're different. You're a girls' dream. You're sweet and kind, and you care. You're not a vampire, not anymore. Clemency knew that. She liked you. And now she's gone missing, and there's blood on her clothes.

Count: Clemency is safe, I am sure. Roderick will find her, or Gunther-Gunther. Soon, I am sure.

Siobhan: You haven't hurt her? Be honest.

Count: I am not sure that I'm still able to inflict harm. I don't want to hurt anyone.

Siobhan: Promise me.

Count: I promise you.

Siobhan: And cross your heart. Like this. (*Crossing her heart*) Like this (*She takes the Count's hand and slowly crosses her heart*).

Count: Siobhan…

Siobhan: Like this. (*Repeating the action*).

Count: My darling. We walk where angels fear to tread.

Siobhan: I love you!

Count: I fear loving you. Half a millennium, and more, without the poetry of love. I have never loved. Nor have I been loved. Cold acquiescence has ever met my passion. If you loved me, I could… Anything. Ask it of me, and I will obey. Siobhan, my most precious possession, for you I would walk in sunlight. (*Crossing to the curtains*) Instruct me! For you, I would throw back these curtains. Without you, I am nothing but a wretched hunger. On your word, I swear, I shall stand beneath Aurora's gaze. This I would do for you-

(*Rebekah enters, carrying a sharpened piece of wood*)

Rebekah: Beelzebub!

Siobhan: (*Screams*)

Rebekah: Spawn of Satan!

Count: Rebekah!

Rebekah: Mephistopheles!

Count: What are you doing? (*Shielded by the sofa and using Siobhan as an extra barrier to Rebekah*) And more importantly, what is that object in your hand?

Rebekah: I am doing the Lord's work, and this is His instrument of justice.

Count: I was afraid you might say something like that.

Rebekah: There is no escape. This tip has been sunk in Holy Water, and soon it shall be sunk in your heart.

Count: Wait. You are making a grave mistake.

Rebekah: Repent!

Count: I realise that Miss Van Helsing's disappearance looks damning.

Rebekah: Repent, I say!

Count: An attractive young lady… (*Siobhan stamps none too gently on his foot with her heel*)… Ouch! Comes to a vampire's castle…

Rebekah: For the last time

Count: But I had nothing whatsoever to do with it.

Rebekah: I was blind, but now I can see!

Count: (*Shouting*) Roderick! Siobhan, you explain.

Siobhan: You had better listen to him.

Rebekah: Has he corrupted you, too?

Siobhan: No… (*Pause*) Not yet.

Rebekah: Speak, Demon.

Count: Roderick. He searches the surrounds.

Siobhan: And he says not to do anything until he gets back.

Count: I'm sure he'll find Miss Van Helsing. He expects to.

Siobhan: She's safe, I bet. Only, playing hard to get. There's a first time for everything.

Rebekah: She hasn't been murdered?

Count: I rather think not.

Siobhan: So you aren't going to spike him. It's best not to. Mr Peters will be mad if you do.

Rebekah: Count, you have two hours until you are at your weakest. At midday, if Miss Van Helsing has not been found I shall strip your body of its breath.

Count: I do so like a compromise.

(*G/G enters*)

G/G: Master?

Count: No need for alarm, Gunther-Gunther, but tell me you are about to offer satisfactory news?

G/G: Telephone. Line severed. Modem destroyed. Wi-Fi down.

Count: A joke? This is a joke, is it? A gag? Who has primed you? Gunther-Gunther, my sense of humour may have atrophied over the centuries, but even I can see that this state of affairs isn't at all amusing. Look, none of us are laughing... deliberately?

G/G: (*Holding aloft a yard of cable*) Found.

Rebekah: Dracula?

Count: Rebekah, let us not act precipitately. I know what you must be thinking. However, I had no prior knowledge of this occurrence.

(*Roderick enters*)

Roderick: Count! What is going on?

Count: I was about to explain to Rebekah how easy it is to misconstrue certain events... probably unconnected. Or that, perhaps, possibly - for some inexplicable reason - somebody is attempting to scare you. Us.

Roderick: They're doing a damned good job.

Count: They are indeed. Gunther-Gunther?

Roderick: (*Pulls phone out*) Why can't I get a signal? I had one last night.

GG: (*To Roderick*) Line cut to modem. Deliberate.

Roderick: The telephone line?

Count: You are no bringer of glad tidings?

Roderick: The cars have been immobilised. Vandalised!

Rebekah: All of them?

Roderick: Even the Count's hearse. Slashed tyres, missing leads, cut pipes. He, she, or it made a thorough, if unsophisticated job of it.

Siobhan: Your Mercedes?

Roderick: Wrecked. Twelve miles to the gallon, that car. Who could do such a thing? Eight, if you put your foot down. Max.

Count: The carriage?

Roderick: No horses.

G/G: *(Happily)* Beyond the castle walls. (**A wolf howls**) Hunger. Fear. Death.

Rebekah: The wolves will tear them to pieces.

Siobhan: It's horrible. They're your pets. Can't you do something?

Count: I wish that I could but, you see, I've… lost the knack. Since… well, recently.

Siobhan: Oh. Mrs Douay?

Rebekah: What is it, child?

Siobhan: Are we trapped here?

(Optional sound effect of three notes: "dun dun dun!")

(Curtains Close)

ACT II SCENE 2

SCENE – *The Sword Room: Later the same day. The curtains open to a room in darkness. The set curtains remain drawn shut.*

Kevin and Debbie, pale-faced, lie sprawled on the settee, dead, their necks bearing the marks of a vampire's bite. Gunther-Gunther enters via the secret door, switches on the room lights and espies the two corpses. Moving across the stage, he inspects them more closely.

G/G: (*Dipping his finger into a trickle of blood, tastes, and nods approvingly*) Masterful, Master. Deceived us all, including faithful Gunther-Gunther.

Rebekah: (*Off stage*) He isn't to be trusted. Nor is his manservant.

(*On hearing Rebekah's voice G/G hastens to turn off the main lights, plunging the set into almost total darkness, and exits through the secret door, closing it behind him*)

Siobhan: (*Off stage*) He says he didn't do any of it.

Rebekah: (*Off stage*) You should flee, both of you. Take the others.

Roderick: (*Off stage*) It's not safe to leave the castle.

Rebekah: (*Off stage*) Is it safe to stay?

(*Roderick, Siobhan and Rebekah enter, dimly lit from behind*)

Roderick: Damn, it's blacker than an oil-slicked cormorant.

Siobhan: We ought to have found Clemency by now.

Roderick: (*Walking cautiously into the room*) Perhaps she's hiding from us. Find the light switch. Perhaps she's the one who wrecked the cars. Lights?

Siobhan: But why? How?

Roderick: How should I know? Damn. (*Stubs his toe on the chair as they all move cautiously about the room feeling for a light*).

Rebekah: The Lord will guide us.

Roderick: I'll settle for a torch. Careful.

Siobhan: Maybe, we should all of us stick together?

Roderick: Unless Clemency is past-tense, and one of us is the culprit?

Siobhan: You're scaring me.

Roderick: Money has been well spent after all. Where's the light switch! Damn!

Rebekah: Tread carefully, Roderick! (*Pause*) Is such treachery possible?

Roderick: Who knows? The Count swears blind that he's innocent. Somebody find the light switch, please. Anyone seen the other two since they decided to go gallivanting around the catacombs?

Rebekah: Our souls may be in peril.

Roderick: My soul's prospects, at this time, do not worry me. It's my skin which I wish to preserve. For Chrissake!

Rebekah: Hold your tongue.

Roderick: Open the curtains!

Rebekah: Here.

(*Rebekah switches on light. Roderick is illuminated about to draw back the curtains. He is stopped by the sound of Siobhan's scream*)

Roderick: Quiet!

Rebekah: Heavenly Father.

Siobhan: Are they dead?

Roderick: (*Bends over the corpses*) As the proverbial.

Rebekah: They are in God's hands. The Count shall not escape me this time.

Roderick: Wait, Rebekah.

Rebekah: I dare not! I have delayed too long already (*Vehemently*) Suffer not a witch to live.

Roderick: Look, Siobhan's right. Maybe we should all stay together.

Rebekah: No, Roderick. Noon approaches and I have been chosen to fight this battle.

Siobhan: So, what are we supposed to do?

Rebekah: Stay here. And put your trust in God.

(Rebekah leaves)

Roderick: (*Shouting after her*) Is that what these two did? (*Pulling a tapestry from the wall and covering the bodies*) Pathetic.

Siobhan: Let's not stay.

Roderick: Shut up. I need time to think. (*To himself*) Rationalise.

Siobhan: I wish we had never come here.

Roderick: Your choice. Now shut it.

Siobhan: I'm scared, Mr Peters.

Roderick: What? What of it, Siobhan?

Siobhan: There's dead people here!

Roderick: So?

Siobhan: A girl has gone missing, probably murdered! All the cars are smashed. Don't you care?

Roderick: I can buy another car.

Siobhan: A car?

Roderick: Listen. We've got to find the Count.

Siobhan: A car!

Roderick: The Count.

Siobhan: Let Rebekah find—

Roderick: Before Rebekah.

Siobhan: Mr Peters?

Roderick: Before Rebekah. We've got to warn him.

Siobhan: I don't understand.

Roderick: Are you stupid? We've got to find the Count before Rebekah does, and warn him.

Siobhan: Why?

Roderick: Because he's important.

Siobhan: He killed Kevin and Debbie. And Clemency, too!

Roderick: Every business has its victims.

Siobhan: You callous bastard.

Roderick: You can't litigate against callousness. The Count is the key to unlocking this whole region. He's a very important man.

Siobhan: He wants to kill you!

Roderick: No he doesn't! And if he does, then perhaps I can offer him something more attractive.

Siobhan: Don't you look at me!

Roderick: Oh, come on, Siobhan. Do I look that callous?

(The Count enters)

Count: Have we found Clemency?

Siobhan: *(Short, sharp scream)*

Count: Siobhan? (*Sees the covered bodies*) Roderick, what is this?

Roderick: Rebekah is coming for you.

Count: And this?

Roderick: See for yourself.

(The Count lifts the tapestry and looks under – aghast but also confused)

Siobhan: You did that!

Count: Those poor creatures.

Siobhan: You did that!

Roderick: Shut it. Count, Rebekah wants to nail your hide.

Count: She… You think that I did this?

Roderick: Personally, I don't give a damn.

Siobhan: You killed them both, and Clemency too, and now he's going to kill us!

Roderick: Siobhan!

Count: Siobhan, this… This appears incriminating - those marks on their neck bear witness to the haemivore's bite - but I don't know how they came to be there. Believe me.

Siobhan: So there's another vampire in the castle that we don't know about? (*Wailing*) Oh, help me!

Roderick: There are no such things as vampires. Siobhan, remember?

Siobhan: Believe your own eyes!

Roderick: A human hand did this!

Siobhan: No! I won't stay here (*Siobhan makes to leave but is restrained by Roderick*).

Roderick: Stop! (*She struggles*) Sit down. Now! Do as you are told! This minute young lady! (*Siobhan petulantly walks to the chair and slumps in it*) OK? (*She nods*) Good. (*To the Count*) I have a way with women.

Count: Rebekah thinks that I am to blame?

Roderick: In one. She believes in all that stuff. We'd better find her.

Count: I know where she will be.

Roderick: Then let's stop her, before she does something that I'll regret.

Count: No, Roderick. You stay with Siobhan. I'll fetch Rebekah back here. Perhaps we can solve this mystery.

Roderick: OK, but be careful. She didn't look receptive to balanced argument. (*The Count makes to leave*) And Count?

Count: Roderick?

Roderick: You and I ought to talk when this is all through. Our unfinished business.

Count: Indeed. Loyalty should be rewarded.

(*The Count leaves*)

Siobhan: Business? Don't you care for anything else?

Roderick: Loyalty should be rewarded.

Siobhan: You can't spend money in Hell, Roderick, which is where that… thing is going to send you.

Roderick: We're going to be partners.

Siobhan: Wake up! (*Getting up from chair*) Two people are dead, still warm, right here in this room, so close that you can smell their fear.

Roderick: And I'm supposed to cry for them?

Siobhan: Don't you care?

Roderick: It's a shame.

Siobhan: Have you no humanity?

Roderick: You cannot rile me.

Siobhan: No? Then maybe I can scare you. Who do you think did this?

Roderick: (*Feigning fear*) Am I going to lose any sleep?

Siobhan: Who did this!

Roderick: Who gives a damn? So long as we live through it.

Siobhan: As long as YOU live through it.

Roderick: It's tough world.

Siobhan: Tell me, Rod, who's going to walk through that door in five minutes?

Roderick: The Count… (*as an afterthought*) and Rebekah.

Siobhan: And Rebekah?

Roderick: Yes, Rebekah.

Siobhan: And then you and the Count are going to talk business?

Roderick: Something like that. He needs me. I'm the linchpin of the project. Without me, it doesn't happen.

Siobhan: Oh, really? So what happens if your ambition isn't as important to him as you think?

Roderick: How could it not be?

Siobhan: Rod, what are you going to do if Dracula walks through that door on his own. (*Silence*) No Rebekah?

Roderick: We can still talk.

Siobhan: And he's going to want to do that, is he?

Roderick: We're going to be partners!

Siobhan: And how many business associates have you thrown to the wolves?

Roderick: Loyalty should be rewarded! You heard him!

Rebekah: (*Off stage, some distance away. A scream*) Heavenly Fatherrrr.

Roderick: Damn! Hell!

Siobhan: Open your eyes, Rod.

Roderick: Vampire's don't exist!

Siobhan: What has made that poor woman cry out? What killed Kevin and Debbie?

Roderick: There are no such things as vampires!

Siobhan: (*Indicating the two corpses*) Then who, or what, did this?

Roderick: There's no man I can't beat.

Siobhan: Is that your ace? Rod, if a human had done this, he'd have needed a sodding vacuum-pump! That's right. Think about it. These two didn't die of fright. Someone, or something, killed them. Someone, or something, has just terrified Rebekah, or worse, and before the day is out, he or it is going to come looking for us.

Roderick: I'm a match for anyone.

Siobhan: Oh, Rod! Not just anyone! (*There is a scratching sound at the door, and the handle begins to turn*) Leave us alone!

Roderick: (*To himself*) Everything is negotiable.

Siobhan: Don't even think about it.

(The door opens. Rebekah stands in the doorway, pale faced, blood at her neck, a wooden stake held loosely in her hand. Roderick rushes forward and holds her before she falls to the floor)

Rebekah: He is the Devil.

Roderick: Damn. Rebekah!

Siobhan: She's trying to say something.

Roderick: Hush! *(Puts his ear to Rebekah's mouth).*

Rebekah: *(Whispers).*

Roderick: I can't hear you!

Rebekah: *(Whispers and dies, spitting a mouthful of blood, the stake falling from her hand).*

Roderick: Christ!

Siobhan: What did she say? *(Silence)* What did she say!?

Roderick: She called my name.

Siobhan: And?

Roderick: Do God's work.

Siobhan: Now do you believe?

Roderick: A vampire?

Siobhan: Yes. God, yes!

Roderick: A vampire. He's a vampire!

Siobhan: Right. So what do we do now?

Roderick: Take our chances. Run for it.

Siobhan: It's more than twenty miles to the village. We'd never make it before nightfall.

Roderick: It's a risk…

Siobhan: No, it's death. The forests are packed-out with wolves.

Roderick: So we stay here?

Siobhan: And what? (*Silence*) And what, Rod?

Roderick: And fight?

Siobhan: Oh yes! I love you.

Roderick: But he's a vampire!

Siobhan: And you're a winner, Rod. Haven't you always been?

Roderick: Do God's work?

Siobhan: Yes. Do God's work. Suffer not a witch to live. Isn't that what Rebekah said? You're the only one who can do it.

Roderick: Me? I'm a stranger in His house. I'm not even sure if I've been baptised.

Siobhan: Then win for us, not for God. For yourself.

Roderick: I'm not sure if I can.

Siobhan: If you don't, we're going to end up like this (*indicating Rebekah*).

Roderick: Look at what he did to her!

Siobhan: No doubts, Rod.

Roderick: He's the strength of ten, isn't that what they say?

Siobhan: Listen to yourself! The man who has never lost a fight.

Roderick: But, Siobhan…

Siobhan: Do it. On your own. I've all the faith you need, Rod. You're the sodding best. Get me through this, and I'm yours. Anything. Anything you want. There's nothing I wouldn't do for you. Anything!

Roderick: For instance?

(Siobhan gives him an exasperated look)

Roderick: Right. Christ, Siobhan.

Siobhan: Will you do it? Huh? Get this monster? For me? For us?

Roderick: Can I?

Siobhan: You must.

Roderick: Damn. Barricade the door *(during the ensuing dialogue the pair move the chair across the doorway. Roderick sits Rebekah on it. Siobhan takes a dagger from the wall and wedges it in the doorjamb)* We'll stay here tonight. Make the place like a fort, so that no-one can get in, and tomorrow morning…

Siobhan: We'll hunt him down.

Roderick: Just like the book.

Siobhan: The bastard.

Roderick: He's going to regret the day.

Siobhan: *(The barricade is completed)* Finished.

Roderick: The French windows! Grab one of those swords. *(Siobhan takes a sword from the wall as Roderick flings back the curtains. Sunlight. The French window bolts are thrown and the sword is slid through the handles)* Impregnable!

Siobhan: Now let him try to get in.

Roderick: Back to the settee!

Siobhan: Rod, pull the curtains shut? I don't want to see when the night comes.

Roderick: *(Drawing the curtains closed)* Done. *(Indicating the far arm of the sofa, nearest to the secret door)* Look, you sit there. I'll sit here, and between the five of us we'll keep him out.

Siobhan: We're safe?

Roderick: We're safe.

(A thick mist begins to seep beneath the door)

Siobhan: Rod? I love you so much.

Roderick: Siobhan.

Siobhan: When we get through this…

Roderick: Let's stay together.

Siobhan: Oh, Rod.

Roderick: For all eternity.

Siobhan: Longer.

Roderick: Are you frightened?

Siobhan: Not anymore. I've no reason to be.

Roderick: You are exquisite. Why did I never see it before now?

(The Count, dressed in the full regalia of the vampire; black clothes, black cape, red lips, sharp teeth, etc enters via the secret passage. A mist swirls at his feet Siobhan - with a yelp of fear - runs to Roderick)

(A crash of thunder, a flash of lightning and a wolf's howl)

Count: Well met, my guests.

Roderick: Well met, yourself.

Count: Ah, Roderick, Roderick. I trust you find my apparel more to your expectations?

Roderick: Black suits you.

Count: Do you think so? For a brief period I sought to immerse myself in different hues, but black does suit me. Yes?

Roderick: It's the absence of any other colour.

Count: And white is a blend of all. Black and white. Darkness and light. Split light in a prism and see the colours of the spectrum, but darkness… darkness has no constituents. Which makes my shade the more pure of the two.

Roderick: You have no purity.

Count: I do believe you've overcome your scepticism, finally.

Roderick: You're real enough.

Count: As you are soon to discover. Siobhan, come here. *(Anguished, Siobhan is impelled towards the Count, but is restrained by Roderick)*

Roderick: *(To the Count)* Stop!

Count: Release her. Roderick, she'll come to me, despite your efforts.

Roderick: Stop! Why? Why all of this?

Count: This? This is what vampires do. And we do it very well.

Roderick: A sophisticated trap? You lured us here?

Count: Not in the least. I genuinely believed I was able to reverse my circumstances. How foolish! I was a capricious alloy, Roderick, forged into a misshapen ideal. Are you aware, I considered having my teeth filed down? But they are me, don't you agree? *(Silence)* Roderick, I so wanted to return to the mortal fold, to regain the lost acceptance of my once-fellow men. But ultimately, I wasn't able. After all, it is not possible to tarnish something that is essentially immaculate.

Roderick: So you killed Clemency?

Count: As with Rebekah, Clemency wanted to destroy me.

Roderick: What happened to her?

Count: Alas, I have no recollection of her despatch. Obviously, her demise can be laid at my feet - or teeth *(chuckles)* but as to how - or precisely when - the deed was committed, I cannot say. To think that I, Dracula, Prince of Vampires, am prone to rages of the blood is frightening.

Roderick: My heart bleeds.

Count: Anatomically imprecise, Roderick. Aim a little higher, as I do. Of course, it was never as frightening for me as this must be for you and the timorous Siobhan. Secured in castle with only a deleterious vampire and his uncooperative manservant for company? If only Debbie were here in a capacity to appreciate it.

Roderick: One day—

Count: A pleasant couple, wouldn't you say? Again, I have no recollection of the deed - which is a pity, as I do so enjoy my repasts - but, again, I'll take the credit.

Roderick: Rebekah, too?

Count: Rebekah? Rebekah had a rush of blood away from her head. Her, I do remember. She was the catalyst that swept the muddled impurities from my heart. Her presumption cast me back into the pit.

Roderick: And now you're there, you like it?

Count: I have a taste for it, now.

Roderick: Very funny.

Count: I wasn't being humorous.

Roderick: And now?

Count: Siobhan is mine.

Roderick: No. I can't let you do that.

Count: Roderick, you have no choice. Siobhan, come here (*Again, Siobhan is drawn to the Count under a strange compulsion*).

Roderick: (*Restraining her. To the Count*) Stop!

Count: I'll let you go, if you give her to me. (*Silence*) Well?

Roderick: Let us both leave. I'll make it worth your while.

Count: Oh, it shall be worth my while. (*Pause*) Roderick, you are attempting to negotiate from a position of precarious insecurity. I suggest that you retire.

Roderick: I can't. It wouldn't be right.

Count: You disappoint me. Moral platitudes from a man of your convictions? Siobhan is your fiancée. I wouldn't have expected such a hollow petition. (*pause*) Roderick, if you don't let her come to me, I shall kill you, nastily. If you release her, I'll ensure that you have safe passage along the forest road.

Roderick: Leave her alone. Please.

Count: Roderick.

Roderick: Let her go.

Count: Last chance.

Roderick: (*After indecision*) Damn you!

Count: She's mine?

Roderick: Yes! Yes!

Count: She always was.

Siobhan: (*Weakly*) Rod?

Rodrick: I'm sorry Siobhan. It's a tough world.

Count: (*To Siobhan*) Walk in my sunlight. (*Siobhan moves to him, fighting the compulsion*).

Siobhan: (*Weakly*) Rod, help me! (*Silence*) I'm scared.

Count: (*Siobhan is almost in his arms*) Do not fear loving me.

Roderick: (*Leaping towards the Count*) Leave her alone!

Act II Sc2 — Jugular Vain

(The fight scene: Roderick and the count battle. Swords and shields should fall off the walls. The action follows loosely the fight outlined by Roderick in Act I Scene 1).

Siobhan: *(Throughout at times of peril)* Rod! Look out! *(Eventually, Roderick is all but beaten, waiting. The count advances on him. As the count looms, Roderick makes the sign of the cross - as in Act I Scene 1 - with his index fingers)*

Roderick: Back! Foul, disgusting, filthy... Leave us, Satan's Advocate! Fly! Into the night on your dark wings...

(The count falls back as Roderick advances. Suddenly, the count reaches out and roughly grasps Roderick's fingers in a single grip)

Roderick: Ouchhhh!

Count: Puny, pathetic creature! Roderick, you are going to have to improve. *(Laughs)* Or die!

(The Count hurls Roderick by his fingers towards the stake Rebekah had dropped on her death. He picks it up. The count snarls).

Roderick: Why not this, hey? Flee now, while you're still able. So help me, I'll run you through...

Count: *(Laughs).*

Roderick: *(Confused)* I wasn't being humorous.

Count: Unwittingly so. *(Proffers his chest)* Here, why don't you?

Roderick: Siobhan? What do I do?

Siobhan: Go on.

(Roderick lunges forward but the Count disarms him easily, takes the stake, snaps it across his knee, catches hold of Roderick and throws him across the settee to the French windows.)

Count: Oh, Roderick. If you could have seen Rebekah's countenance. You're fools, all of you. Exactly like Clemency's ancestor. WHO DO YOU THINK HELPED STOKER WRITE THE BOOK?

(**A crack of thunder. A wolf howls**)

Roderick: Oh, God!

Count: Not even close, Sir. It was I. And was I ever likely to disclose my Achilles heel? (*Pause*) One more hollow victory, but they do suit me so. And now, Roderick, Siobhan is going to watch you die.

(*The Count advances, Roderick struggles to his feet and, as the Count looms, he turns and pulls back the curtains, flooding the vampire in sunlight*)

Count: (*Falling back, snarling*)

Roderick: Roast! Roast!

Count: (*The Count's cry of pain turns to ringing laughter*) It's a sad thing, redundant imagination. Rebekah threw Holy Water at me! (*Sighs*) Au revoir, as we cosmopolitan types say.

Roderick: Siobhan! Help me! (*The Count is almost upon him*)

Siobhan: How? (*Pause*) The sword! Cut his head off! The sword!

Count: (*Snarls*)

Siobhan: Yes! That's it!

(*Roderick takes the sword from between the handles of the French windows*)

Roderick: Au re-Bleedin'-voir, Count. (*Menacingly advancing*) You're about to receive a lesson in anatomy.

(*The Count pauses at the secret door*)

Count: Beware the darkness, Roderick. (*The Count exits*)

Slobhan: After him!

Roderick: (*At the secret door*) Siobhan, when this is all over…

Siobhan: I know. You're going to mess me around and leave me for a woman five years younger.

(Curtains Close)

ACT 2 SCENE 3

SCENE – *The Sword Room: Night. The curtains in front of the French windows are open, admitting moonlight. The set is devoid of people. The corpses of Kevin, Debbie and Rebekah are missing. The door to the secret passage has been shut. The other door is partially open, and the settee is partially askew.*

Roderick enters via the main door, bloodied, pushing the chair fully back. He is carrying a bloodied sword, snapped in half. In his other fist he holds a handful of dust.

Roderick: (*Weary, dropping the sword*) Siobhan? Siobhan? (*He looks out through the French windows*), Babe? Siobhan? (*To himself*) Look at me. (*Allowing the dust to trickle through his fingers*) Look at him. Six-hundred-year-old fish food. Instant Vampire - just add water… and a head. (*Pause*) Siobhan? I wonder if they'll let me into Heaven after this?

Eradicating a vampire? Dead cert. I could sin until I'm ninety and they'd still let me in. Except… I don't much feel like sinning, anymore. I feel … OK. Good. Terrific, even. I've just thrown away the biggest resource management deal since the rainforest was invented and, yes, I feel great. Odd! What would the environmentalists think of me now? Roderick Peters, Pollution Control. (*Kicking the dust on the carpet*) This… this is pollution. Moral pollution. Where's the book? The Count's address book? I've done it once; I can do it again. And again.

Roderick Peters, Vampire Hunter. This is great! I'll protect the world from vampires. But why stop at vampires? I'll protect the world from Roderick Peters. No more hardwood desks. No more strip mining. No more deals. The gas-guzzlers and the turbos, I'll have them converted to hybrids. I'll buy a Tesla - well maybe not. I'll sell them all. Travel by rail. Get a bike! What else? No more looking through the tins of tuna for lumps of dolphin. I'll put the right-coloured glass in the bottle bank, and take the boxes home. Snuff out the waste-incinerator ship. I'll shut the cadmium mines and the palm oil refineries. Someone else can dump toxins in Africa, but if I catch them… Someone else can ship ponies to France. I'll set up a fox sanctuary, the little beauties.

(Loudly) Oh! I love this world!

Siobhan: *(Off stage, from the secret passage)* Mr Peters? Roderick?

Roderick: Siobhan! In here!

Siobhan: Roderick? I've got the book!

Roderick: Honey! It's Rod, in here!

Siobhan: There's no light.

(A mist begins to seep beneath the secret door)

Roderick: Stay where you are. I'll open the door.

Siobhan: It' so dark.

Roderick: Any second… *(Roderick look curiously at the mist swirling about his feet)* Siobhan! Hold on! *(To himself)* How did he do this? *(Moments later, Roderick locates the mechanism which operates the door)* Siobhan?

(Siobhan enters, stepping through the mist. She is dressed in a long black dress, is pale-faced and has blood-red lips. She is a vampire.)

(A crash of thunder, a flash of lightning and a wolf's howl)

Siobhan: Well met, Roderick.

Siobhan: Siobhan? Siobhan?

Siobhan: Roderick.

Roderick: What are you…? I don't understand?

Siobhan: Look at me, you fool. *(As Siobhan in Act I Scene 3)* Vampires who live forever. No growing old, no waiting for that first wrinkle. No wilting breasts, or slack thighs, or painful joints. No hair shot with grey. *(As Siobhan, the Vampire)* The Count and I, we are the same. Kindred spirits. Or at least we were, until you dispatched him with your gallant innocence.

Roderick: You're a vampire?

Siobhan: If shrewdness were longevity, Rod, you'd live to be a hundred. Unfortunately, it isn't. And you won't.

Roderick: You're really a vampire?

Siobhan: Oh, dear. I have been for a good - or should I say bad - number of years. I enjoy it. I kill people. I feed off them and they die.

Roderick: No!

Siobhan: Yes. Dracula, he was like me. Once.

Roderick: Until I destroyed him.

Siobhan: For which you have my eternal gratitude… and my transient appetite.

Roderick: (*Picking up the sword*) Dracula, he was the best of them, but I conquered. What's to stop me doing the same?

Siobhan: My new companion.

(G/G enters from the passageway, gun in hand, book in the other)

G/G: (*Passing the book to Siobhan with a low bow*) Madam.

Siobhan: (*Flicking through the pages through the short monologue*) Is this what you want? (*Silence*) Drop the blade, Roderick. (*Silence*) (*Looks up briefly*) Now! (*Silence*) (*Sighs*) Do you really want to embrace oblivion without knowing why I came here? (*Silence*) Roderick, let go of the sword, or Gunther-Gunther (*who cocks the pistol*) will shoot you… (*as an afterthought*) in the legs, to begin with. Or perhaps the groin. The magazine holds, I believe, twelve bullets.

Roderick: (*Throwing aside the sword*) Why?

Siobhan: Because that's how many it holds…

Roderick: No, I meant why all this?

Siobhan: Dracula's 'Renaissance'. The Prince of Darkness, running a Bed & Breakfast? Eating carrots? Donating to charity? I couldn't allow it. Vampires exist for no other reason than to be vampires. We are the one percent. Immoral elitism.

Roderick: The Count didn't kill Clemency, did he?

Siobhan: All my own work.

Roderick: Your work that included the deaths of Kevin and Debbie?

Siobhan: Their faces! Like two rabbits in headlights just before they go beneath the wheels. Surprise! Oh, yes. An amusing thing; for all their talk, they would have like to have died a peaceful death, of old age, in their sleep. Just like you do. (*Laughs*) Fun, Roderick, fun.

Roderick: You're sick, disgusting.

Siobhan: I'm a vampire. Clemency, the Lovely Couple, the cars the telephone wire, all my own doing. To goad Dracula into renouncing his conversion. He'd be forced to recant, to resume the mantle of vampirism and you, Roderick, would fight in order to preserve your own pitiful existence. Roderick, the unassailable sceptic. Until Rebekah fell dead at your feet. I knew it would take something of that magnitude to stir your sleeping wit. You fought Dracula, not as man against man but as good against evil, and I gave you the edge. (*As timid Siobhan*) The sword! Cut his head off! The sword!

Roderick: Why?

Siobhan: Ah you can't guess?

Roderick: (*A pause*) A vampire cannot kill another?

Siobhan: A gem, isn't it, omitted from Stoker's novel.

Roderick: With Dracula out of the way…

Siobhan: I'm the Queen Vee. If the cape fits, Roderick, wear it. I have the book, the castle, Gunther-Gunther…

G/G: (*Nods and bows again*) Madam.

Siobhan: Gunther-Gunther is no longer disheartened. 'White Vampires' are a forgotten whim. (*Holding aloft the address book*) This, this is the key to a resurgence in active vampirism. Names and numbers. My vision and their determination. More bites, more clients - to use the phrase of yesterday's ghoul - more vampires. Proliferation, Roderick. Shadows across the earth. (*Pause*) Beginning with you. Fancy yourself as a one-in-a-hundred?

(*Clemency opens the French windows. She is pale-faced, red lipped. Her nightclothes are wet, bloodied and bedraggled*)

Clemency: He may not, but I do. (*She lingers at the threshold*)

Siobhan: Darling! Do come in!

Clemency: (*Crossing to Siobhan and palming her off*) Don't darling me, bitch. Hello, Roderick.

Roderick: What is this?

Siobhan: This is an unexpected delight!

Clemency: I figured you'd be happy. (*To Roderick*) That gorgeous Count and I stayed up until 3am this morning. Just chatting, learning about each other, getting quietly horny, that sort of thing. When, finally, I turn in… guess who's waiting for me in my room? You have it in one. Suddenly, I come over all peculiar, and before I could say no, or maybe, or perhaps yes, (*looking seductively at Siobhan*) this lady is touching me up and sucking the life-blood from my veins. Bitch. Still, it was fun though. The next thing I know, she's tipping me into the moat, tied to a rock. I felt like I was resting. No light, no sound, just the caress of the cold water, or the gentle eddy of a passing current. Soft and dim. Later, I half-woke and struggled to the surface. Not long ago. And here I am.

Siobhan: You're my first.

Clemency: And you were mine.

Siobhan: Hungry, darling?

Clemency: Famished.

Siobhan: *(To Roderick)* Come here. Now! Do as you are told! This minute old man! *(Roderick is compelled to move forward)* Good. *(To Clemency)* Enjoy. He'll not resist. I have a way with men.

Clemency: And I'll have my way with men.

Roderick: *(As Clemency and Siobhan close in on him)* Clemency! *(Bellows)*

(Curtains Close)

(THE END)

Furniture, Property List & Effects Plot

On Stage:

    Sofa
    Chair
    Bookcase with at least one book that is used as secret door mechanism
    Table with drinks / 3 x decanter / glasses
    Various swords, shields and tapestries as wall dressings
    One Sword, a dagger and a tapestry that can be removed from their fittings and used
    A portrait of a vampire (above fireplace)

Off Stage:

    Smoke Machine
    Bloodied sword / snapped
    A yard of telephone cable – roughly cut
    Ladies dressing gown – torn and bloodied
    Women's purse with various ID documents within
    Cobwebs for Rebekah's hair
    "Antique" leather-bound book
    Dust / Vampire's remains
    Pondweed and water
    Pistol
    Oversized bandages / smaller bandages / plasters

Personal:

    Roderick: Smart phone
    Clemency: Silver cross necklace, smart phone
    Rebekah Large wooden cross / stake

Lighting effects:

    Sun and moonlight to come through French windows.
    Single spotlight for Count's soliloquy / with semi-blackout on rest of stage

Sound effects:

    Wolf howl (various)
    Owl hoot
    Thunder rumble (long and short)
    Thunder crack (long and short)

Published by Leschenault Press
Leschenault, Western Australia

www.ingramcontent.com/pod-product-compliance
Lightning Source LLC
Chambersburg PA
CBHW041147110526
44590CB00027B/4153